ANTI-SOCIAL BEHAVIOUR

SAGE SWIFTS

In 1976 SAGE published a series of short 'university papers', which led to the publication of the QASS series (or the 'little green books' as they became known to researchers). Almost 40 years since the release of the first 'little green book', SAGE is delighted to offer a new series of swift, short and topical pieces in the ever-growing digital environment.

SAGE *Swifts* offer authors a new channel for academic research with the freedom to deliver work outside the conventional length of journal articles. The series aims to give authors speedy access to academic audiences through digital first publication, space to explore ideas thoroughly, yet at a length which can be readily digested, and the quality stamp and reassurance of peer-review.

ANTI-SOCIAL BEHAVIOUR

A MULTI-NATIONAL PERSPECTIVE OF THE EVERYDAY TO THE EXTREME

CATE CURTIS

SAGE SWIFTS

$\circledS$SAGE

Los Angeles | London | New Delhi
Singapore | Washington DC | Melbourne

$SAGE

Los Angeles | London | New Delhi
Singapore | Washington DC

SAGE Publications Ltd
1 Oliver's Yard
55 City Road
London EC1Y 1SP

SAGE Publications Inc.
2455 Teller Road
Thousand Oaks, California 91320

SAGE Publications India Pvt Ltd
B 1/I 1 Mohan Cooperative Industrial Area
Mathura Road
New Delhi 110 044

SAGE Publications Asia-Pacific Pte Ltd
3 Church Street
#10-04 Samsung Hub
Singapore 049483

© Cate Curtis 2016

First published 2016

Library of Congress Control Number: 2016930558

British Library Cataloguing in Publication data

A catalogue record for this book is available from
the British Library

Editor: Chris Rojek
Editorial assistant: Delayna Spencer
Production editor: Vanessa Harwood
Marketing manager: Michael Ainsley
Cover design: Jen Crisp
Typeset by: C&M Digitals (P) Ltd, Chennai, India
Printed and bound by CPI Group (UK) Ltd,
Croydon, CR0 4YY

ISBN 978-1-4739-1577-0
eISBN 978-1-4739-3388-0

To Edmond Knops and Jeanne Knops-Janssen

A timely work given the present global shift in the use of social media and violence. Cate Curtis' book serves as a multinational mini-meta-analytic review of anti-social behaviours. Each chapter builds developmentally by topic to the concluding chapter that outlines various intervention alternatives. This is a book that will fit well in both undergraduate and graduate courses in psychology, family studies, education (social justice), social welfare, nursing, criminal justice, political science, behavioural economics, sociology, and anthropology.
Richard Langford, University of Hawaii West Oahu

In seven chapters, *Antisocial Behaviour* neatly and succinctly takes readers through ways to understand and interpret the label of 'antisocial' behaviour in a wider context, showing how it is socially, historically and culturally produced as well as understood in professional health and policing or correctional contexts. In her innovative Swift intervention, Curtis also grapples with new forms of antisocial behaviour as imagined in online spaces, and examines the new ways in which communities and governments have sought to police, 'correct', or limit this type of behaviour. The text offers a crisp insightful synthesis of core issues in social psychology.
Cathy Coleborne, University of Newcastle, Australia

Cate Curtis' coverage in this book on anti-social behaviour is breath-taking. It is centred on challenging taken for granted assumptions concerning the three Rs: 'risk', 'resilience' and 'recovery' whilst questioning what is respectable everyday activities and extreme behaviour in culture and society. Her investigation into social behaviour is fast paced and detailed assessing diverse and oppositional arguments as she moves towards a complex assessment of multiple factors, which shape the meaning of anti-social behaviour. Written in an accessible style with scholarly depth, the book will be touchstone for students and researchers in sociology, criminology, media and cultural studies, politics and social policy.
Shane Blackman, Canterbury Christ Church University, New Zealand

CONTENTS

ABOUT THE AUTHOR

Cate Curtis (PhD) teaches social psychology at the University of Waikato, New Zealand. Following an earlier career in the NGO sector, she remains passionately interested in the well-being of young women. Her research includes the construction of risk and resilience and women's self-harm. She has also published on socio-economic factors in suicidal behaviour, public perceptions of the forensic use of DNA and research methods.

ACKNOWLEDGEMENTS

I am grateful to SAGE staff, particularly for their patience. Many others have also contributed to this book, some through their faith in me, some by practical support and others by stimulating a desire to prove them wrong. You know who you are, and I thank you all.

ACKNOWLEDGEMENTS

I

INTRODUCTION

Anti-social behaviour is a topic of widespread interest in the Western world, as shown by the number of media reports, academic articles, government policies and legislative changes. Anti-social behaviour (as it is most often concept-ualised and discussed) is most common during adolescence and, depending on how it is defined, is estimated to involve 5 to 17 per cent of young people in the Western world. Young people are disproportionately implicated in minor crime, which overlaps with anti-social behaviour; in the UK it is estimated that youth crime costs more than one billion pounds per year (The Prince's Trust, 2010); this figure includes the cost of imprisoning young people, estimated at £587 million in 2009. In the US, approximately $6 billion is spent on imprison-ing young people (Puzzanchera & Sickmund, 2008); around a quarter of a million people aged under 18 years are prosecuted through the adult criminal justice system each year. A spike in youth offending during the 1980s and 1990s triggered laws to refer more young people to adult court, harsher sen-tences for some crimes and lowering of the age at which a child could be prosecuted as an adult. Policymakers believed these efforts would deter future crime. However, anti-social behaviour encompasses far more than criminal behaviour. Though difficult to define, it may include everything from minor nuisance behaviours that would not be considered problematic by some to the perpetration of major harm to many people. In addition to the degree of harm enacted, intention must also be considered.

Anti-social behaviour, and sub-topics including "risk", "resilience", "juvenile delinquency", "intervention" and "justice", can only be understood if the socio-political context in which these terms are used is understood. These terms and the issues they connote exist relative to matters such as professional and political agendas; public (mis)perceptions; and social, economic and political change. Reactions to anti-social behaviour are not simply based on increases in this behaviour. For example, as discussed by Hendrick (2006), governments continually devise policies to deal with the "new" malaise of youth crime in an attempt to return to the "good old days", yet there is nothing new about youth crime, and the notion of "the good old days" is contestable, to say the least. Nonetheless, we need a start point of shared understanding, and discussing definitions of anti-social behaviour seems a logical place to begin.

This first chapter introduces anti-social behaviour, including its legal and clinical (International Classification of Diseases (ICD); Diagnostic and Statistical Manual of Mental Disorders (DSM)) definitions as well as the various definitions used and assumed in the media and general public understandings. The approach taken to "anti-social behaviour" in this book is discussed along with an introduction to the book itself.

DEFINITIONS

"Anti-social behaviour" as a specific problem requiring specialised solutions is a notion that has evolved in the past 20 years in Britain and thereafter in Commonwealth and/or European countries (though there have been similar objects of concern such as "out of control" teenagers in the 1950s). Definitions of anti-social behaviour vary and are often vague, broad or both.

In the UK, the use of the term may be associated with New Labour. For example, in the preface to the *Respect Action Plan*, the "heart" of the problem of anti-social behaviour is described by then Prime Minister Tony Blair as "a lack of respect for values that almost everyone in this country share – consideration for others, a recognition that we all have responsibilities as well as rights, civility and good manners" (Respect Task Force, 2006, p. 1). This concern can also be seen filtering through to the UK public:

> There is an increasingly high emphasis being placed by the Government on antisocial behaviour (ASB) and methods to tackle it. This is particularly evident through the setting up of the Antisocial Behaviour Unit (ASBU) ... the Antisocial Behaviour "Together" Action Plan and ... the Antisocial Behaviour Act during 2003. Antisocial behaviour is a key issue of public concern. A count of reports conducted by ASBU in England and Wales in September 2003 found that over 66,000 reports of antisocial behaviour were made to agencies on one day. The 2003/04 British Crime Survey (BCS) shows that over a quarter of the public perceive particular behaviours such as vandalism, graffiti, litter and teenagers hanging around as a problem in their local area. (Home Office Development and Practice Report, 2004, p. 1)

The British Home Office developed a typology of anti-social behaviour comprising four key categories, each with numerous examples. These four categories are: misuse of public space; environmental damage; disregard for community/personal well-being; and acts directed at people (Home Office Development and Practice Report, 2004). It seems noteworthy that only one of these categories refers to acts deliberately targeted at another person, yet anti-social behaviour is associated with a great deal of public concern and political attention.

Anti-social behaviour may not necessarily involve criminal activities – and to some extent this depends on the policies of any given jurisdiction, such that what is considered a crime in one country may not be so in another; or indeed, though technically a crime, it may be the case that there is a reluctance to prosecute. This will be discussed further in the next chapter. It is noteworthy that the 2003/04 British Crime Survey BCS mentioned above discusses public concern about littering and "teenagers hanging around", for example.

The term "anti-social behaviour" is used somewhat differently in various (anglophone) countries. In particular, it appears that in the US the term is used predominantly with regard to pathology, as in anti-social personality disorder (which will be discussed below). The term "anti-social behaviour" as used in the UK has no precise equivalent in the US; depending on the context, "juvenile delinquency" or "civil disorder" may come closest. As noted by Bartol and Bartol (2009), in the US these terms may be used interchangeably by stakeholders, along with the psychological terms "conduct disorder" and "externalising problem behaviour". In contrast to these psychopathological associations, it could be argued that "anti-social behaviour" as used in the UK has a more politicised meaning and is linked to criminalisation. The question of the appropriateness of criminalising or pathologising will be returned to in Chapter 3.

A common sense lay definition of anti-social behaviour is "behaviour which is deemed contrary to prevailing norms for social conduct, or behaviour contrary to the laws and customs of society, in a way that causes annoyance and disapproval in others" (Oxford University Press, 2015). One definition from the US is "a cluster of related behaviors, including disobedience, aggression, temper tantrums, lying, stealing, and violence" (Eddy, Reid, & Curry, 2002, p. 27). The website "US Legal" describes anti-social behaviour thus:

> Antisocial behavior is behavior that misses out consideration for others and that may cause intentional or negligent damage to society. It is the opposite of pro-social behavior which helps or benefits society. Both criminal and civil laws offers remedies for antisocial behavior. Antisocial behavior can begin in childhood, adolescence, or adulthood. In children it is referred as conduct disorder and it can be

identified when the child is as young as three or four years of age. And, in adults, it is referred as antisocial personality disorder. A person who exhibits antisocial behaviors will be extremely selfish and self-centered. Adults that are affected by antisocial behavior might … get involved with white collar crime. (US Legal, 2001–2015)

Despite the website having that name, this does not appear to be a legal definition and assumes a pathological basis while also allowing for legal "remedies" and moral judgements. The Western Australia Police define anti-social behaviour as any "behaviour that disturbs, annoys or interferes with a person's ability to go about their lawful business" (McAtamney & Morgan, 2009, p. 1), though it is acknowledged that defining anti-social behaviour is difficult due to variations with regard to how communities define what is anti-social based upon perceptions of problems in their community; in other words, anti-social behaviour is socially constructed and culturally relative.

As discussed by Millie (2009), a vague definition runs the risk of failing to give fair warning to the public of what is, and is not, illegal and also poses problems for those seeking to understand anti-social behaviour. However, it has been argued that there are advantages to having a flexible definition from a political perspective; it can range from minor nuisance behaviours as mentioned above (further examples include failing to maintain one's garden, or driving a noisy car) through to serious harassment and criminal activity, while from a legal perspective, it is claimed that a broad definition allows for the prioritisation of the concerns of particular communities. It may also have advantages for NGOs funded to provide services such as prevention and intervention programmes (this will be discussed further in Chapter 7). Nonetheless, operational definitions that may be used in a legal context exist.

According to the British Anti-social Behaviour, Crime and Policing Act, "anti-social behaviour" means –

(a) conduct that has caused, or is likely to cause, harassment, alarm or distress to any person,
(b) conduct capable of causing nuisance or annoyance to a person in relation to that person's occupation of residential premises, or
(c) conduct capable of causing housing-related nuisance or annoyance to any person.

This replaces the Crime and Disorder Act (1998) definition of anti-social behaviour: "Acting in a manner that caused or was likely to cause harassment, alarm or distress to one or more persons not of the same household as (the defendant)" (Home Office Development and Practice Report, 2004, p. 2).

Thus, anti-social behaviour may be conceptualised as a nuisance activity that may or may not be illegal. It might also be considered to have a pathological basis. The World Health Organisation (WHO, 2015) includes anti-social behaviour in the ICD as "dissocial personality disorder", a

> personality disorder characterized by disregard for social obligations, and callous unconcern for the feelings of others. There is gross disparity between behaviour and the prevailing social norms. Behaviour is not readily modifiable by adverse experience, including punishment. There is a low tolerance to frustration and a low threshold for discharge of aggression, including violence; there is a tendency to blame others, or to offer plausible rationalizations for the behaviour bringing the patient into conflict with society.

The diagnosis of dissocial personality disorder is reserved for adults. The ICD description of conduct disorder, which is applied to adolescents and children, is rather more detailed:

> Disorders characterized by a repetitive and persistent pattern of dissocial, aggressive, or defiant conduct. Such behaviour should amount to major violations of age-appropriate social expectations; it should therefore be more severe than ordinary childish mischief or adolescent rebelliousness and should imply an enduring pattern of behaviour (six months or longer). Features of conduct disorder can also be symptomatic of other psychiatric conditions, in which case the underlying diagnosis should be preferred.

> Examples of the behaviours on which the diagnosis is based include excessive levels of fighting or bullying, cruelty to other people or animals, severe destructiveness to property, fire-setting, stealing, repeated lying, truancy from school and running away from home, unusually frequent and severe temper tantrums, and disobedience. Any one of these behaviours, if marked, is sufficient for the diagnosis, but isolated dissocial acts are not.

As well as various exclusions, there are a number of variations of conduct disorder, including socialised and unsocialised conduct disorder; conduct disorder confined to the family context; depressive conduct disorder; oppositional defiant disorder; other mixed disorders of conduct and emotions, and unspecified conduct disorder.

The American Psychiatric Association, in the fifth edition of its DSM (2013), provides criteria for the diagnosis of persistent anti-social behaviour in adults over the age of 18 as anti-social personality disorder. In those aged under 18, the corresponding diagnosis is conduct disorder. The essential features of a personality disorder include impairments in personality functioning (both with regard to oneself and interpersonal functioning) and the presence of pathological personality traits.

The specific diagnostic criteria for anti-social personality disorder are rather too long and detailed for the scope of this book, but key elements include:

- Pathological personality traits in the following domains: antagonism, characterised by, for example, manipulativeness and hostility, and disinhibition, characterised by impulsivity, irresponsibility or risk-taking.
- Significant impairments in personality functioning, demonstrated by impairments in self-functioning, such as self-esteem derived from power, personal gain or pleasure; and impairments in interpersonal functioning including empathy or intimacy. These impairments are relatively consistent and stable and are not better understood as normative for the individual's socio-cultural environment or developmental stage.
- The impairments in functioning and the personality trait expression are not solely due to a medical condition (e.g., severe head trauma) or the effects of a substance (e.g., drug abuse, medication).

In conduct disorder, a persistent and repetitive pattern of behaviour occurs in which major age-appropriate societal norms or the basic rights of others are violated. To be eligible for this diagnosis, the behaviour must cause "clinically significant" impairment in academic, social or occupational functioning. Conduct disorder is significantly more likely to be diagnosed in boys than in girls, with a lifetime prevalence rate of approximately 2.4 boys to every girl. It is also more stable in boys. Diagnosis includes time-limited criteria, with the presence of at least three of the following (which have been simplified for the purposes of this book):

- Aggression to people and animals – for example, bullies or intimidates others; initiates physical fights; has been physically cruel to people or animals; confrontational theft; forced sexual activity.
- Destruction of property.
- Deceitfulness or non-confrontational theft, lying to obtain goods or favours or to avoid obligations.
- Serious violations of rules, such as frequent truancy.

THE APPROACH TAKEN TO "ANTI-SOCIAL BEHAVIOUR" IN THIS BOOK

This book goes beyond many of the common definitions that are often focused on pathological and/or criminal behaviour, especially committed by young men, but often at a low level of severity. This book, therefore, broadens the discussion to include the extremes of anti-social behaviour, such as hate crimes and terrorism, as well as interrogates understandings of anti-social behaviour, such as the belief that anti-social behaviour is increasing in young women, while critically examining the risk factor paradigm. Part of that broadening is to include transnational perspectives – from across the English-speaking world and Europe; material from elsewhere is included where appropriate, bearing in mind significant cultural differences.

Much of the material which informs this book arose in the UK; it is supplemented by material from Europe, my home country New Zealand and nearest neighbour Australia; I also include the US, though as mentioned above the term appears to be used considerably less frequently, and when used, it is usually linked to psychopathology (as in "Anti-social Personality Disorder"). As mentioned above, the nearest terms appear to be "juvenile delinquency" and "civil disorder" though they may be rather narrower conceptualisations and cannot be considered equivalent. Much of the behaviour included is criminal, but the criminalisation of some forms of anti-social behaviour will also be examined.

Although the importance of historical background is acknowledged, given the broad coverage of this book, contemporary or continuing issues will be the focus. Other key social and contextual factors such as class, gender, culture and ethnicity are integrated into the chapters as appropriate, in particular (but by no means exclusively) in Chapters 2 and 3. It is not possible to include all areas of behaviour that may be broadly considered anti-social; for example, domestic/intimate partner violence is not included. The focus is on actions that potentially impact people *outside* the immediate family, in accordance with definitions that explicitly exclude household members.

BOOK OVERVIEW

The study of anti-social behaviour, in its various forms, falls within the ambit of criminology, social psychology, sociology and social work. This book draws upon both foundational writings and recent research from all of these fields. Understandings of anti-social behaviour are not only the domain of academia; they are also of interest to the general public as well as to members of the public sector, such as policy analysts, and those involved in the justice and social welfare systems. The aim of this work is to synthesise and summarise current knowledge across academic disciplines in an accessible manner. This means that some of the key concepts introduced in the next chapter will, of necessity given the broad audience, appear elementary to those with a background in the relevant field, but will be new to other readers.

The term "anti-social behaviour" carries with it some assumptions about behaviours, perpetrators, victims and impact, while also frequently being defined poorly. Over recent years (particularly in the UK), it has often been associated with problematic behaviour engaged in by young people, which may or may not be criminal. This aspect of anti-social behaviour will certainly be covered thoroughly, including perpetrator risk and resilience factors, prevention and intervention. The intention here is to go beyond individualised discussion to explore broader concepts such as the social construction of "anti-social behaviour", "risk" and "resilience", and the social contexts and influences under which these factors are more likely to occur. In addition, a broader approach to anti-social behaviour itself will also be taken, exploring the gamut of anti-social behaviour. In doing so, key theories and concepts from the social sciences will be applied, such as strain theory, social learning theory, social identity theory, differential association, labelling theory, deindividuation, moral panics and issues of social control. Issues of politics, gender and the role of new media (e.g., cyber-bullying; the use of social networking sites to foment and display anti-social behaviour) are also included. Rather than treating issues of gender and cultural context as separate from the core topics, these are fundamental to each and as such are integrated throughout.

An overarching theme of the book will be the interrogation of notions of "risk" and "resilience". There is a substantial body of research on "risk" and its association with anti-social and criminal behaviour. However, there are significant problems with the risk factor approach, in particular in regard to the way conceptions of risk and resilience are socially constructed, as the analysis of risk and protective factors is often undertaken in the absence of their historical, social and cultural location (Armstrong, 2002).

This book will begin by establishing the context for the study of anti-social behaviour, including definitions and parameters, before moving on to explore the ideologies and epistemologies underpinning "anti-social behaviour". Various forms of "anti-social behaviour" will then be explored, from the everyday (e.g., minor nuisance behaviours) to the extreme. In the concluding chapter, these threads will be drawn together and applied to the examination of common intervention and prevention strategies.

Building on the definitional issues introduced in this first chapter, Chapter 2, "Perceptions and concepts: Constructing anti-social behaviour", will discuss the social construction of "anti-social behaviour" and related topics. In this chapter, early models and related foundational theories will be surveyed. These include the work of Freud, Durkheim, Merton, relevant evolutionary theories and social models such as Bandura's social learning theory. More recent key ideas, such as those that emerged during the 1960s and 1970s, the work of Tannenbaum, Becker and Foucault, through to the current debates that include the role of risk factors and the notions of risk and resilience, are also included. In addition to the discussion of social and cultural variations in perceptions of anti-social behaviour, the role of biology, including a brief discussion of genetic predisposition and the impact of neurology, particularly neurotransmitters, will be included – though the focus of this book is on the social aspects of anti-social behaviour. Thus, a background to the major underpinning concepts is provided.

Armstrong (2004) argues that concerns about youth risk and crime reflect personal anxieties, competing social values and public policy rather than issues of risk and resilience per se. In a number of Western countries, offending by young people has declined significantly since the 1990s, alongside a decrease in reported victimisation, and most crimes are committed by adults. However, the public significantly overestimates the extent of youth crime. Armstrong further argues that the plethora of policy initiatives focused on "at risk" youth (in the UK) is the corollary of a moral panic about out-of-control children. These constructions, perceptions and concepts form the basis for the third chapter, "The politics of anti-social behaviour: Policies and values".

The fourth chapter, "Ordinary anti-social behaviour: Everyday hassles", will examine some of the more common forms of anti-social behaviour, such as "nuisance behaviours" (e.g., street loitering, aggressive driving), bullying, and graffiti. Relevant theories are applied, such as social identity theory, and common underlying factors, including parenting practices and alcohol use, will be explored both at face value and from a critical stance. For example, in many Western countries, parents are increasingly held accountable for the behaviours of their children, particularly when such behaviours transgress laws. Neglectful and abusive family environments are clearly detrimental to well-being and may be linked to anti-social behaviour. However, neglect and abuse often occur within a transgenerational cycle and are enacted in negative social environments (see, e.g., Bower-Russa, Knutson, & Winebarger, 2001). A decreased sense of control for parents, which may manifest as neglect of their children, may be due to social factors such as precarious employment and inadequate housing.

Many forms of anti-social behaviour have a social element. While gang activities are an obvious example, there are many others ranging from relatively minor schoolyard bullying to large-scale organised activity, including genocide, at the extreme. Key concepts of the fifth chapter, "Anti-social behaviour as a social activity: Group processes", include situational influences, the development of stereotypes, conformity and the development of "hate-groups".

In this chapter, the relevant theories to be applied include diffusion of responsibility and deindividuation and social identity theory to understand how these group behaviours are initiated, explained and maintained.

The sixth chapter is "New technology, new media: Transmitting new anti-social behaviour?". Considerable public concern appears to exist about an increase in some forms of anti-social behaviour, such as text and cyber-bullying, while other new technologies may provide means of inciting group behaviours, for example, through the use of social media. In addition, the increasing level of violence in entertainment, particularly computer games, has become a topic of debate, with links drawn between media violence and increased aggression. The evidence for such claims and counterclaims is discussed, along with appropriate theories and explanations such as habituation and desensitisation. It is argued that the availability of new technologies has given rise to new forms of anti-social behaviour; however, current areas of concern are misplaced.

Crime reduction strategies have tended to focus on individual, psychogenic and family-related antecedents in the immediate social environment of the individual, rather than in the wider community or socio-political structures. The focus on risk factors offers a management system based on identifying/blaming "dysfunctional families" while justifying surveillance and intervention. The implication is that control is lacking, echoed by public and media calls for punishments such as "boot camps" and harsher (particularly long-term custodial) penalties for those who engage in anti-social behaviour. In the final chapter, "Prevention and intervention: Risk, resilience and recovery", approaches to prevention, intervention and punishment of anti-social behaviour are discussed. Links to the earlier discussion of politics are made and the impacts and effectiveness of common methods are overviewed, for example, forms of early (at or prior to school entry) identification and intervention; "boot camps"; and restorative justice. Though a comprehensive discussion of psychopathology is beyond the scope of this book, treatments for conduct disorder and anti-social personality disorder are touched upon.

The book concludes with some observations on the creation of anti-social behaviour. These include the continued relevance of early theories of deviance and identity and the need for further attention to social and structural factors. The creation of situations in which anti-social behaviour is relatively normal, even adaptive, is emphasised.

2

PERCEPTIONS AND CONCEPTS: CONSTRUCTING ANTI-SOCIAL BEHAVIOUR

Building on the definitional issues introduced in the first chapter, the social construction and evolution of "anti-social behaviour" and related topics are discussed in this chapter. As mentioned previously, due to the transdisciplinary nature of this book, it is necessary to "do the groundwork" for the rest of the book by briefly covering key concepts from across disciplines; therefore, some material will be very familiar to some readers, while for others it will be new. In order to give some historical background to current perceptions, the chapter begins with an overview of early models and related foundational theories, such as those of Durkheim, Freud and Merton. More recent key ideas are included, such as those that emerged during the 1960s and 1970s, including the work of Bandura on social learning and that of Tannenbaum, Lemert and Becker on deviance and labelling. Classic psychological studies of obedience and conformity are mentioned, before touching on Foucault's ideas about social control.

A further focus of this chapter will be the construction of risk factors along with protective factors and the related topic of resilience, though the former will also be discussed in the next chapter with regard to the politics of risk. Though the focus is largely on the social, the role of biology is briefly over-viewed; such as genetic predisposition. Finally, public perceptions of anti-social behaviour will be discussed.

Although anti-social behaviour is currently perceived as a serious social problem and is usually near the top of the political agenda of Western countries, definitions of anti-social behaviour are somewhat problematic. There are some common themes, but definitions vary across history, country and context. Millie (e.g., 2009) refers to Durkheim's notion of the "collective conscience": what defines a criminal (or anti-social) character is not intrinsic, but derives from the collective conscience of society. When clear behavioural norms are absent, such as during a time of social or economic change, there is a state of anomie (alienation, relative normlessness or lack of regulation). This raises the question of whose norms are given primacy; after all, it may well be the case that those who engage in anti-social behaviour are behaving within the norms of their peer group or sub-culture. Beginning with Durkheim, the following section provides an overview of the development of related concepts such as deviance, conformity and social control over time.

Emile Durkheim indirectly proposed that in industrialised societies containing social hierarchies based on economic or relational merit, anti-social behaviour is increased. In *The Division of Labour in Society* (1893 (1984 translation)), Durkheim coined the phrase "anomie". Anomie may be understood as social disorder of a breakdown between the individual and the social, derived from a mismatch between individual actions and broader social norms. Further, "The more one has, the more one wants, since satisfactions received only stimulate instead of filling needs" (Durkheim, 1951 (original work published 1897), p. 248). It follows from this that human desires can only be held back by external controls. Society imposes these controls in the form of norms. If the norms of a society are unknown, transgressed or absent, anti-social activity can flourish. Thus, Durkheim effectively proposed a sociological theory of anti-social behaviour. Robert K. Merton took Durkheim's work further to assert that social structures exert pressure upon some individuals to engage in non-conforming rather than conforming behaviour (discussed below).

Though overlapping chronologically, at first glance Freud's work may appear to have little in common with Durkheim's. Although Freud did not directly theorise about norms, social structures or anti-social behaviour, both Durkheim and Freud were concerned with human behaviour and, in particular, transgression of accepted boundaries. Freud thought that human behaviour, including aggressive behaviour, was the product of "unconscious" forces operating within the mind. In this view, behaviour that lies outside societal acceptability, including the anti-social, is the result of abnormal development of the psyche. In classical Freudian theory, the psyche is determined by early childhood experiences; therefore, the roots of anti-social behaviour are also to be found in this period, particularly in the relationship between the child and his or her caregivers. For Freud, aggression was therefore a fundamental human impulse that is repressed in the majority of well-adjusted people who have experienced a normal childhood. However, if the aggressive impulse is either insufficiently controlled or repressed excessively, some aggression may "escape" from the unconscious and random acts of aggression and anti-social behaviour may result. Freud referred to this as "displaced aggression" (Englander, 2007). Though he was by no means a sociologist, we can draw parallels between Freud's concept of individual (or psychic) strains which result in anti-social behaviour and Merton's work on structural strains in society as a basis for deviancy.

Along with strain theory, Merton is perhaps best known for creating the term "self-fulfilling prophecy", a key element of social psychological, political and sociological theory. Self-fulfilling prophecy refers to the situation in which the expectation of a person (especially a third party) influences the way a person will behave or the outcome of a situation; for example, a teacher's expectation of bad behaviour and corresponding treatment of a student may increase the likelihood of bad behaviour from that student. In general, Merton's work in relation to anti-social behaviour can be thought of as an attempt to adapt Durkheim's ideas about anomie to specific social situations, especially Merton's (1938) analysis of the relationship between structure, culture and anomie. For Merton, "anomie" meant a disjunction between social goals and the means available for achieving them. In this respect, Merton altered Durkheim's con-cept of anomie, from a situation in which norms are relatively absent (it may be argued that true normlessness is impossible and beyond what Durkheim meant) to one in which individuals may experience anomie if they are *unable* to abide by the norms, or achieve the goals, of society. Merton argued that society, especially American society, was structured in such a way that the vast majority of people could not reach the expected, or socialised, goals for behaviour. The result is the occurrence of anomie because of the strain between what people have been socialised to desire and what they are legitimately able to achieve. An explanation for both conformity and deviance is thus provided.

Edwin Sutherland (1924) developed the theory of differential association at around the same time as strain theory. This theory held that the development of criminality arises from association with those who commit crime; as such, it has some commonalities with the work of Bandura (discussed below): crimi-nal behaviour is learned in interaction, as a social process. This learning may include specific techniques as well as attitudes and justifications. The theory also initially had a broader social aspect in that conflict and social disorgan-isation underlie crime because they determine patterns of social interaction. Sutherland remained interested in social class as a factor in crime and is credited with first using the phrase "white-collar criminal".

Initial traces of the concept of criminalisation may be found in sociology of the 1930s, especially in the work of Frank Tannenbaum. Considered the grandfather of labelling theory, Tannenbaum (1938) argued that deviance, rather than being the behaviour of an individual, can only be created through a process of social interaction. In *Crime and Community* (1938), he described the social interaction involved in crime, arguing that although many may engage in deviant acts, only a minority come to be recognised as deviant. This "deviant" is then categorised and treated as such, even though their behaviour may be the same as others'. As a result, certain people are constructed as and "become deviant" through social judgements of their behaviour.

Edwin Lemert (1951) further developed Tannenbaum's ideas by differentiating between primary and secondary deviance. Primary deviance is often an isolated transgression which is not related to a self-identification as deviant. Secondary deviance occurs as a result of the reaction of others to the initial deviance. Through stereotyping and labelling by others, a deviant identity is adopted, and one's attitudes and behaviours are adapted accordingly; deviance and conformity result from how others respond to actions, rather than the actions themselves. Lemert considered all deviant (or anti-social) acts to be social acts, a result of social interactions which initiate a psychological process concerning one's own identity and the subsequent adoption of and justification for anti-social behaviour. Lemert's (1967) conclusion that social interaction, especially social control, causes deviancy was a pivotal point, politicising the study of deviance, crime and social control (Muncie, 2007a).

Though Lemert introduced the key concepts of labelling theory, Howard Becker became the theory's advocate. For Becker too, the origins of deviance and anti-social behaviour lay in the reactions of others rather than in the behaviour itself. Rather than a pathological act that transgressed accepted norms, deviance is created through micro-level interactions between the transgressor and others.

> Deviance is not a quality of the act the person commits, but rather a consequence of the application by others of rules and sanctions to an "offender". The deviant is one to whom that label has successfully been applied; deviant behaviour is behaviour that people so label. (Becker, 1963, p. 9)

Thus, some people come to be defined as deviants, whereas others – who have not been subject to these interactions – do not. Further, Becker considered the attached stigma to be crucial in the development of future deviant or anti-social behaviour; a self-fulfilling prophecy follow the stigma of, and identification with, the label. This emphasis shifted attention from the behaviours of "deviants" to those who perceive those behaviours as problems (Muncie, 2007a).

In Albert Bandura's work, we can see the coming together of the social and the individual foci. Bandura is best known for social learning theory (also known as social cognitive theory): learning is a cognitive process that occurs in a social context and takes place through explicit instruction or the observation of norms of behaviour, even in the absence of direct reinforcement. Bandura's (1973, 1977) research included analysis of the willingness of children and adults to imitate others' behaviour, in particular, aggression. He found that in addition to observing others' behaviour, learning also occurs through vicarious reinforcement: the observation of rewards and punishments received by others. Thus, Bandura's theory goes beyond traditional behavioural theories, by emphasising the roles of various internal processes in the individual, over and above reinforcing rewards and punishments.

In 1960, Bandura, with Dorothea Ross and Sheila Ross, conducted what became known as the "Bobo doll experiment", showing that children base their own behaviour upon models (in this case, adults who behaved aggressively towards a "Bobo doll"). When the adult models were praised for aggression, the children were more likely to be aggressive and indeed, to invent new forms of aggression. However, when they observed the models being punished, the children ceased their aggression towards the doll. The results were highly influential in psychology, helping to shift the focus from pure behaviourism to cognitive psychology. Many of Bandura's innovations came from his use of empirical and replicable investigation, which were foreign to a field of psychology dominated by the theories of Freud.

While on the topic of mid-century social psychology, mention must be made of the work of Stanley Milgram, Solomon Asch and Muzafer Sherif (see, e.g., Asch, 1951; Milgram, 1963; Sherif, 1958; Sherif, Harvey, White, Hood, & Sherif, 1961). Motivated by the events of WWII, their research aimed to understand obedience and conformity through questions such as "Why do we go along with the group, even when we disagree?"; "In what circumstances will we obey orders that go against our own morals and values?". Findings included the importance of the presence of an authority figure; the perceived norms of the specific situation or group; the number and behaviour of others present; including observers, colluders and dissenters. In all of these experiments, we can see tensions between self-governance and social influence.

Foucault noted that from early modernity, European society evidenced increasing concern with social control as a practice of government (in the sense of governing others' behaviour and governing one's own). He (1979) described this as disciplinary social control because of the reliance on the observation, training and control of individuals to improve them, whether to transform criminals into law-abiding citizens, new recruits into disciplined soldiers, or patients into healthy people. He argued that the purpose of this discipline and social control is to render individuals docile; disciplinary social control is a key to the creation of a normalising society. When norms, rather than legal mechanisms, are used to govern our lives, society can be said to be controlled through socialisation and normalisation. This stands in contrast to the use of formal justice procedures which are used only when laws are broken (Little & McGivern, 2014).

Donoghue (2008) observes that while the works of Foucault and of Donzelot (1980) in particular have examined the crucial disciplinary role exercised by welfare and social workers in controlling populations, including those implicated in anti-social behaviour, Rose (1985), Garland (1985) and Squires (1990) have examined the interchange between those interventions relating to welfare, care and protection and those relating to control. These issues will be discussed further in the next chapter. More recently, Parr and others have argued that the social constructionist approach prevalent in post-Foucauldian governmentality concepts is limited and would benefit from the critical realist lens. This would assist progression beyond description and deconstruction of discourses to further explain underlying material realities (Parr, 2009).

Contemporary debates and research include the evaluation of risk factors and their role in prevention; resilience and protective factors; notions of risk and resilience more broadly and their critique (though such critiques will be included in the next chapter); and the prediction of adolescent-onset versus life-course persistent offenders.

RISK FACTORS

In this section, risk factors will be discussed, beginning with macro-social and moving to the individual. It should be noted that (unsurprisingly) exposure to multiple risk factors increases the likelihood of engaging in anti-social behaviours. However, the area of risk and resilience has been a topic of increasing concern over recent years, in part as a corollary of concern over anti-social behaviour. As mentioned in the previous chapter, although there is a substantial body of research on risk with regard to anti-social behaviour, significant problems with the risk factor approach remain, in particular in regard to the way conceptions of risk and resilience are socially constructed. Further critique of the risk factor paradigm, and of the notion of resilience, will be included in the next chapter.

Structural or Societal Factors

We can see an interaction of class, ethnicity, economic adversity and "justice" interventions in the overrepresentation of indigenous young people in the justice systems of Australia, New Zealand and Canada, and African-Americans in the US, for example. White and Cunneen (2006) argue that institutionalised racism, which includes the distribution of resources, labelling and victim-blaming as well as targeting of specific groups by a punitive justice system, is at the heart of much anti-social behaviour, especially that engaged in by marginalised youth.

Low socio-economic status appears to predict anti-social behaviour, though some (e.g., Farrington, 2015) would argue that this seems to be because parents in these situations have poor parenting skills and/or significant personal and social problems. Conversely, it could be argued that socio-economic disadvantage creates situations in which positive parenting is difficult to maintain, for example, because of stress, long hours of work and so forth.

Neighbourhood Factors

At the neighbourhood or community level, urban living, disadvantage and disorganisation (e.g., changes in state welfare and housing policies, poverty, resident mobility and low social cohesion) are linked to high rates of anti-social behaviour. However, it is unclear whether living in these communities increases anti-social behaviour or that people at risk of anti-social behaviour live in these areas due to limited life chances, given that they are likely to be suffering from a range of disadvantages.

Discussed further in the next chapter with regard to the "broken windows theory", it may be that living in neglected neighbourhoods creates a norm of disrespect or lack of care for others. These neighbourhoods may also be considered in Durkheimian terms as engendering anomie. Regardless, such neighbourhoods are characterised by a lack of opportunity.

Interpersonal Factors

A variety of aspects of the interpersonal context are implicated in anti-social behaviour, as defined by most of the academic literature. These include family circumstances and the influences of peers.

Family factors

An insecure attachment style, whether ambivalent or avoidant, is associated with anti-social behaviour. In particular, parental negativity and rejection is linked to externalising behaviours such as disruptiveness and aggression (Kochanska & Kim, 2012); indeed it appears to be the case that the parent–child relationship is characterised by *mutually* adversarial communication and behaviour, building resentment and hostility (Kochanska, Barry, Stellern, & O'Bleness, 2009). This links to the oft-replicated finding that poor parental supervision is a reliable predictor of offending (as discussed by Farrington, 2015, among others). In addition to the poor relationship itself, poor attachment may generalise to other relationships, leading to a failure to identify with values and norms regarding obedience, and insufficient development of internal control, alongside a negative attitude to authority. Of course, there may be any number of underlying structural and social factors that impinge upon parental ability to provide supervision, such as working long hours as well as the parents' own individual issues.

Although many studies have shown a link between broken homes and anti-social behaviour, obviously most young people from broken homes do not engage in particularly problematic behaviour. Factors that increase the likelihood appear to be parental discord, many changes of primary caregiver and separation from a biological parent before the age of 10 (Farrington, 2015). Family conflict and violence in general are established risk factors (Ireland & Smith, 2009). Unfortunately, the child from a dysfunctional home is more likely to miss potential positive influences elsewhere.

Having a teenage mother also appears to increase risk, though this is influenced by changes in caregivers, maternal characteristics such as intelligence, and other family factors including harsh discipline, disruption and parenting styles (Jaffee, Caspi, Moffitt, Belsky & Silva, 2001). These, in turn, may be the result of a lack of social support and financial resources (and therefore may be mediated by the provision of such resources and support).

Anti-social behaviour appears to be a common characteristic of some families. As discussed with regard to Bandura's social learning theory, harsh or physical punishment models coercive and aggressive behaviour, establishing such actions as normal strategies for dealing with challenging situations. In addition to intergenerational transmission, which may be based on any of the social factors mentioned above as well as genetic predisposition, anti-social behaviour frequently occurs in siblings.

In addition to the somewhat more severe family factors mentioned above, a general milieu lacking in positive experiences is associated with anti-social behaviour; this may include lack of engagement on either the part of the young person or the family (often developing into a reciprocal pattern); few positive family activities; a lack of involvement in family activities on the part of fathers; and a lack of clear rules.

In sum, family factors influence poor parenting and anti-social behaviour in a number of ways, including parental absence and disruption, poor or non-existent parental relationships and the impacts of poverty. These families are often characterised by harsh or inconsistent discipline, limited positive interactions and poor attachment.

The Influence of Peers

Anti-social behaviour results in, and may also be caused by, rejection by the "normal" peer group, and in the case of young people, the reinforcement of pro-social behaviour is likely to be absent at home and possibly school and other social contexts. Having peers and friends who engage in anti-social behaviour is strongly associated with engaging in anti-social behaviour oneself; this is particularly true of those aged under 18, who are to engage in anti-social behaviour with others. Those aged over 18 are more likely to act alone or begin to withdraw from anti-social behaviour (see Hemphill, Heerde, Herrenkohl, & Farrington, 2015, for a brief review and further reading). The influence of peers will be discussed further in Chapter 5.

Gender and Anti-social Behaviour

Concerns about an apparent increase in (young) women engaging in problematic behaviour, more typically seen as "men's" behaviour, such as excessive alcohol consumption, physical fights and crime, have been increasing, alongside some arguments made that it is the result of gender equality (Adler, 1975; Simon, 1975). Though some of these concerns date back decades, thorough research into the topic is rather sparse.

In many countries, the rate of imprisonment of women has increased disproportionately over recent decades. This may be understood as a corollary of the feminisation of poverty: social factors such as an increase in single-parent families, the concentration of women in poorly paid jobs, gender roles which place the burden of care of dependents on women (thus reducing opportunities for paid work) and neo-liberal policies which have resulted in the stagnation or reduction of wages and salaries and of welfare assistance in real terms may underlie increasing anti-social behaviour and thus increasing imprisonment of women. This increase in economic marginalisation may be linked to girls' and women's increased involvement in dishonesty, such as shop-lifting and benefit fraud. An unanticipated outcome of the feminist movement may also be at play; Adler discussed the "dark side of women's liberation" which may be applied to "ladette" behaviour. While there have certainly been some changes in gender roles for young women (also discussed in relation to girls in gangs; see Chapter 5), there appears to be clear evidence for a correlation between public policy, anti-social behaviour and women's imprisonment. Morash (2006) gives examples from the US and UK; with regard to the UK, she draws a link between cuts to youth wages and welfare benefits and prostitution, alongside rhetoric around imprisonment or confinement in state facilities for girls' protection.

The supposed increase in women's criminal behaviour is most dramatic with regard to serious crimes and violence, including more use of weapons. Despite this, there has been little investigation of the underlying reasons. However, it has been argued that men and women who engage in anti-social behaviour have similar social profiles: low socio-economic status, dysfunctional family background, abuse, poor educational achievement, un(der)employment and belonging to a minority ethnic group (Murdoch, Vess, & Ward, 2011; Steffensmeier & Allan, 1996). It would appear that women who engage in violence frequently have a history of sexual abuse, view violence as normative and have a negative view of themselves, others and the world in general (Murdoch, Vess, & Ward, 2010).

Conversely, Rennison (2009) argues that there has been almost no change in the violent crime gender gap in the US if age and race are taken into consideration; results clearly point to gender stability regardless of the race or age of the offender. In the rare cases where there has been a statistically significant difference, it was due to a greater decline in male offending rates compared to the decline in female offending rates.

The early onset of puberty is linked to anti-social behaviour (and depression and a range of other negative outcomes) in girls (Caspi & Moffitt, 1991). However, this is moderated by context; for example, girls at mixed-sex schools appear to be more at risk than girls at single-sex schools. This may be due to difficulty maintaining friendships with same-age peers due to salient physical differences, association with older peers who may have different norms, increased risk of sexual assault and of substance use, and lower academic achievement (Mendle, Turkheimer, & Emery, 2007).

Further, Merlo and Chesney-Lind (2015) convincingly argue that maltreatment and abuse of girls is at the heart of an increase in the arrest and imprisonment of girls, presenting the US data on the prevalence of "dual status" girls (girls who have been both victims and offenders) in the justice system. This argument has some similarities to that of Murdoch, Vess, and Ward (2011; see Chapters 3 and 7, this volume) with regard to violent offenders in New Zealand. Based on this argument that the failure to protect girls from harm is related to increased anti-social behaviour, Merlo and Chesney-Lind conclude with a programme that focuses on reducing harm in order to prevent future offending.

Masculinity, femininity and alcohol

Recently the role of alcohol use in conforming to ideas of masculinity, and contesting ideas of femininity, has been explored. Public and excessive consumption of alcohol with other men has long been a traditional indication of masculinity in many Western cultures. However, over recent decades, this association has been eroded, partly through increased alcohol consumption by women (McCreanor et al., 2013; Willott & Lyons, 2012). Griffin, Szmigin, Bengry-Powell, Hackley, and Mistral (2013) argue that femininity is profoundly contradictory, calling for young women to be independent but not "feminist"; to look and behave "sexy" but not be "sluts"; and to drink but not to "drink like men". While it appears that men have achieved greater choice (though mediated by class), women's freedom and empowerment in this regard is largely illusory.

Individual Factors

Individual risk factors for anti-social behaviour may be broken down further into socio-psychological and biological factors, though there is often an overlap between the two, or a combination of socio-psychological and biological is indicated.

Poor school achievement is often found in those who engage in anti-social behaviour (Farrington, 2015). While this has often been linked to low intelligence or cognitive deficit, it may be an artefact of social factors, such as non-attendance, a lack of valuing of education by peers or family or difficulty concentrating for a variety of reasons such as poor nutrition, tiredness and problems or distractions at home. Impulsiveness or attention deficit hyperactivity disorder (ADHD) may also be factors. Nonetheless, an association between poor educational achievement and anti-social behaviour has been demonstrated repeatedly (Hemphill et al., 2015).

Psychological factors

Gottfredson and Hirschi (1990) developed self-control theory (a "General Theory of Crime") in the early 1990s. Based on the observation of a consistent connection between criminal behaviour and age, they theorised that the most important factor underlying crime is an individual's lack of self-control. They further argue that self-control is determined solely through socialisation processes, especially those that occur in the family, such as parental management practices, rather than by biological and genetic influences. Individual self-control improves with maturity as a result of a range of factors, including changing hormonal levels, socialisation and the increasing costs of losing control. In addition, criminal acts are often clearly non-controlled; they are impulsive, short-sighted and opportunistic.

There is considerable evidence for the role of impulsivity in anti-social behaviour, and it may be regarded as the most strongly related individual factor (see, e.g., Farrington, 2015; Hemphill et al., 2015; Higgins, Kirchner, Ricketts, & Marcum, 2013). However, there are many constructs that are related to impulsive behaviour, such as poor ability to delay gratification, sensation-seeking, hyperactivity and low self-control. At least some of these also have biological components, as will be discussed below.

Depression is also linked to anti-social behaviour, especially among girls (Cook, Pflieger, Connell, & Connell, 2015; Ritakallio, 2008; Teplin et al., 2006), as are some other psychological disorders, including anxiety and post-traumatic stress disorder (Tillfors, El-Khouri, Stein, & Trost, 2009; Vermeiren, Deboutte, Ruchkin, & Schwab-Stone, 2002), although the relationship to anxiety is less clear and appears to be related to other factors such as the presence of ADHD and the early onset of anti-social behaviour (Hodgins, De Brito, Chhabra, & Côté, 2010; Polier, Herpertz-Dahlmann, Matthias, Konrad, & Vloet, 2010).

Developmental perspectives

Psychological research over recent decades has tended to focus less on personality traits and developmental (including cognitive) aspects of the individual and, to some extent, their social context. Bronfenbrenner's (1979) ecological (or nested) systems theory was a key influence which emphasised the importance of environmental factors. However, most developmental theories take an individual approach.

Classic studies have identified some important factors in the developmental trajectory of a person who engages in anti-social behaviour. Terrie Moffitt's work has been particularly influential, but other classic studies include those of Robins (1978) and Patterson, DeBaryshe, and Ramsey (1989). It would appear that the younger the age at which anti-social behaviour is exhibited, the more stable and severe it is likely to be; adults who exhibit anti-social behaviour will usually have exhibited clear signs in their childhood. These children probably missed potential positive influences elsewhere: they may have frequently missed school, be in the care of welfare authorities and therefore less likely to be with "normal" peers or involved in sports or other structured activities. "Late starters" are less likely to continue, probably because they missed the early social causal factors. That said, according to Robins' work, most children who engage in anti-social behaviour do not continue into adulthood. These features generally fit well with Moffitt's adolescence-limited versus life-course persistent taxonomy.

Despite its dominance in literature on the development and progression of anti-social behaviour, Moffitt's (1993) taxonomy of "adolescence-limited" and "life-course persistent" anti-social behaviour has not been without critics (see, e.g., Skardhamar, 2009; Stattin, Kerr, & Bergman, 2010). Anti-social behaviour is most often engaged in during adolescence, but those who begin their anti-social "career" during childhood are more likely to persist into adulthood. Moffitt argues that once young people are able to take on the legitimate responsibilities of adulthood, most will do so; therefore their anti-social behaviour is limited to adolescence. However, Moffitt also argues that a small number of adolescent-onset individuals become "ensnared" by addiction, imprisonment or other circumstances that lead to their anti-social behaviour continuing across the life-course. McGee and colleagues (2015) sought to further examine these snares using Australian data and found that this group is significantly more likely to have been raped, been through a court process, and experienced unemployment, substance abuse and neighbourhood disorder, and often a combination of these. Early parenthood and dropping out of school early were not implicated – indeed some research (e.g., Giordano, Seffrin, Manning, & Longmore, 2011; Kreager, Matsueda, & Erosheva, 2010; Monsbakken, Lyngstad, & Skardhamar, 2013) suggests that parenthood can precipitate desistance from anti-social behaviour, especially for young women.

Moffitt postulated, apparently correctly, that her theory would be applicable regardless of race or ethnicity with regard to adolescent-onset anti-social behaviour, but that disadvantaged ethnic groups would be at greater risk of life-course-persistent issues (Moffitt, 1994, 2006).

Biological Explanations
Though psychological factors may have biological associations, such as abnormal levels of neurotransmitters and stress hormones, they are typically considered issues of the psyche. There are also factors that may be conceptualised primarily biologically. These include sex hormones and genetics.

Biological explanations – sex hormones
Hormones are one biological factor that may impact upon anti-social behaviour and the gender difference in engagement. Testosterone is correlated with aggressive behaviour in both men and women, though levels are typically higher in men. However, causation is unclear; it may be that aggression increases testosterone production (Morash, 2006). Boys are more commonly diagnosed with ADHD which appears to be linked to impulsivity and anti-social behaviour and may have biological influences. Although recent research on the biological bases of anti-social behaviour provides some evidence for reasons why boys and men tend to be more anti-social than girls and women, such predispositions are one factor of several.

Biological explanations – genetics

While a growing body of empirical research suggests that genetic factors are implicated in anti-social behaviours, evidence is also emerging which indicates that environmental factors moderate the effects of genetic factors. However, much remains unknown. Increased exposure to criminogenic risk factors, such as having peers that engage in anti-social behaviour and low social support, increases the impact that genetic factors have; environmental risk factors exacerbate pre-existing genetic tendencies towards anti-social behaviours, and without these environmental factors, genetic propensity remains unlikely to be realised. As environmental factors are more readily changed than genetic factors, it is logical that environmental risk factors be the focus of intervention and prevention programmes. It would appear that genetic factors are also relevant to victimisation (Beaver, 2011; Beaver, Boutwell, Barnes, & Cooper, 2009), though this is outside the scope of this book.

RESILIENCE AND PROTECTIVE FACTORS

Many resilience or protective factors (also sometimes called promotive factors) are simply the opposite of risk factors; for example, an authoritative parenting style is a protective factor (whereas a neglectful parent presents a risk), as is a positive school environment. An influential grandparent or inspirational youth or social worker may act as a protective factor. As with risk factors, resilience and protective factors may be individual or environmental in nature, and there is frequently an interaction between the two. The presence of these factors may lead to increased self-efficacy, appropriate levels of self-esteem, realistic future aspirations and a positive self-concept in general.

PUBLIC PERCEPTIONS

Despite the attention paid by academia, policymakers and politicians, public perceptions of anti-social behaviour are unclear, although there is some suggestion that anti-social behaviour policy may have increased negative stereotypes of youth (Bannister & Kearns, 2013). As discussed by Egan, Neary, Keenan, and Bond (2012), there is a need to consider whether public concerns about young people's anti-social behaviour are motivated by a response to actual anti-social acts or subjective perceptions arising from other factors. A study of neighbourhood disorder in the US found that compared to measures of disorder derived from independent observations, factors such as neighbourhood deprivation and ethnicity strongly influenced perceived disorder.

Many contextual factors, at macro-, local and individual levels, appear relevant. Egan and colleagues' research in the UK found some evidence of negative attitudes, such as generalised stereotyping of young people, but not a broader climate of intolerance. Results showed that the heterogeneity of young people and their behaviours was recognised, suggesting that while adult residents of disadvantaged communities perceive young people's anti-social behaviour to be a serious issue, they recognise that such behaviours occur in a social context, are grounded in situational factors and involve a minority of individuals (Egan et al., 2012). It is also worth reiterating that, despite having a broad definition of anti-social behaviour, nearly three-quarters of the British public do not appear to perceive anti-social behaviour to be a problem (Home Office Development and Practice Report, 2004).

In the Netherlands, members of the public are quoted as fearful and calling for increased government action (van der Leun & Koemans, 2013). As illustrated in a quote from the British Home Office above and discussed further in the next chapter, public views of "street terror" are used by politicians as a justification for punitive policies, following claims that disorder and nuisance have grown out of hand in disadvantaged areas and that local citizens call for action. New measures have been introduced in the Netherlands, some of which are very similar to British tactics like the anti-social behaviour order (ASBO). However, a comprehensive study involving a range of stakeholders in several Dutch cities shows a relatively nuanced and varied range of perceptions (van der Leun & Koemans, 2013).

Nonetheless, perceptions of anti-social behaviour may not be linked to experience or witnessing such behaviour. Higher levels of fear are associated with an increased tendency for individuals to withdraw from community life, ultimately resulting in the atomisation of local communities and a decrease in social cohesion (creating a self-fulfilling prophecy). People adjust their behaviour to avoid fear-inducing areas, especially at certain times of the day. By thus limiting their exposure to risky situations – *and therefore anti-social behaviour* – they may report fewer such behaviours subsequently (Brunton-Smith, 2011).

With regard to public attitudes to responding to youth anti-social behaviour and crime specifically, Jones (2010) argues that despite low levels of knowledge of crime rates, options for dealing with anti-social behaviour, and the outcomes of these options, cross-national surveys suggest a punitive attitude among the general public of many Western countries, with a desire for retribution being common. It may be argued, therefore, that punitive policies are a response to the demands of citizens. However, little appears to be done to educate the public.

CONCLUSION

Theorists from across the social sciences have contributed to the understanding of anti-social behaviour. These include theories about social and psychological strains, norms, the impact of labelling, the construction of deviance and other social influences. Although some of these are reflected in our current conceptualisations, at this point in time, there tends to be a greater focus on individual than on social and structural factors.

Although a range of risk factors from the structural to the individual are recognised, policy initiatives and justice interventions also tend to focus on the individual or, in some cases, on their family (as will be discussed further in Chapter 7). This individual focus is problematic as it may be used to target individuals, potentially leading to unjust criminalisation. This targeting may also be in response to public (mis)perceptions and stereotypes. The political context in which responses to anti-social behaviour occur is the focus of the next chapter.

3

THE POLITICS OF
ANTI-SOCIAL BEHAVIOUR:
POLICIES AND VALUES

Concerns about anti-social behaviour, risk and crime are not based on accurate perceptions but on socially constructed and personal anxieties, conflicting social and cultural values and political machinations. In a number of Western countries, offending by young people has declined significantly since the 1990s, alongside a decrease in reported victimisation. However, the public significantly overestimates the extent of youth crime and anti-social behaviour. Thus, it may be argued that a political focus on anti-social behaviour, especially that of young people, stems from a moral panic.

Anti-social behaviour is, of course, nothing new, as seen in examples (translated or modernised) from texts dating back centuries:

> I would there were no age between sixteen and three-and-twenty, or that youth would sleep out the rest; for there is nothing in the between but getting wenches with child, wronging the ancientry, stealing, fighting. (Shakespeare, "A Winter's Tale", sixteenth century)

> I see no hope for the future of our people if they are dependent on frivolous youth of today, for certainly all youth are reckless beyond words ... When I was young, we were taught to be discreet and respectful of elders, but the present youth are exceedingly wise [disrespectful] and impatient of restraint. (Hesiod, eighth century BC)

> The young people of today think of nothing but themselves. They have no reverence for parents or old age ... They talk as if they alone knew everything and what passes for wisdom with us is foolishness with them. As for girls, they are forward, immodest and unwomanly in speech, behaviour and dress. (Attributed to Aristotle c. 330 BC)

❮❮

Using Cohen's (1973) classic analyses of social control, it is possible to reveal the extent to which the construction and control of anti-social behaviour is characterised by the shifting of boundaries and competing ideologies (Brown, 2004). This chapter interrogates the ideological and political underpinnings of beliefs about anti-social behaviour. For example, behaviour deemed to denote risk is often more visible in poor communities, but there are multiple possible constructions of why this is. There is no doubt that anti-social behaviour does bring high social and economic costs to many communities, and the concerns of those communities deserve to be taken seriously. The purpose of this chapter is to examine the politics underlying responses to anti-social behaviour, to question the assumptions embedded in "risk" and to critically evaluate the impact of related responses and policies. This includes a discussion of moral panics, the risk factor paradigm, and power, control and inequality. In doing so, this chapter enhances the possibilities for developing responses that are effective for all stakeholders.

In modern times, "juvenile delinquency" first emerged as a public and political concern during WWII – as a result of wartime disruption. Alongside a lack of young men, and especially fathers, boys were perceived as unruly and undisciplined. In the 1950s, reports of normal community-based social behaviour, such as street football, were seen as positive, a sign of life returning to normal. Now street football, or young people (especially young men) congregating in public places, is often seen as "risky" and tantamount to anti-social behaviour.

Over the post-war years in the UK, policy and practice moved from a focus on welfare and treatment towards punishment as the key for addressing anti-social behaviour, culminating in New Labour's Crime and Disorder Act of 1998. In the UK, the ASBO was promoted as a key element of the "fight against anti-social behaviour and the promotion of a 'respectful' society".

> Worklessness, serious drug and alcohol misuse, even involvement in crime can become associated with problem behaviour. Where parents are involved, that can place their children at serious risk ... I am pleased that an ASBO is now a household expression – synonymous with tackling antisocial behaviour. We needed a radical step change and we got one – ASBOs, dispersal orders, crack house closures. All radical, all getting the decisions taken on the front line, all fast and effective and all welcomed out there in communities. There is good work being done by local communities to apply this approach to tackle unacceptable behaviour. 6,500 ASBOs, 13,000 acceptable behaviour contracts, 800 dispersal orders and over 500 crack house closure orders have been issued, while provisional figures show over 170,000 penalty notices for disorder have already been issued. But there is a huge amount still to do. (Tony Blair's foreword: Respect Task Force, 2006, p. 1)

ASBOs were introduced in England and Wales in 1999, and similar "tools" have been introduced elsewhere since. ASBOs are civil orders ostensibly designed to protect the public from behaviour that causes or may cause harassment, alarm or distress – though this behaviour might not be criminal; and breaching an ASBO is a criminal offence. An order prohibits the offender from specific acts or entering certain areas for a minimum of two years. The orders are not intended to punish the offender and, according to the Home Office, should not be viewed as an option of last resort. However, they frequently constitute "naming and shaming" with names and photographs published on council websites and the like. They are intended to encourage local communities to become actively involved in reporting anti-social behaviour and protecting the community. The civil nature of the order meant that both hearsay and professional witness evidence can be included in proceedings (Youth Justice Board & Home Office, 2003). However, the ASBO can also provide a useful case study of policy that has not lived up to its promise.

ASBOs have not delivered the reduction in anti-social behaviour that was anticipated, and in fact it may have increased, as shown by a Home Office research in 2003. A number of criticisms have been levelled, including that it is a distraction from the failure of the government's law and order policies, an opportunity for institutionalised vigilantism, and is a symbol of punitive populism. There is little restriction on what can be designated as anti-social behaviour or on what a court may impose as the terms of the ASBO, and very few ASBO applications have been refused; in fact a Freedom of Information Act request (Ministry of Justice, 2014) shows that between 1 April 1999 and 31 December 2013, 9,651 ASBO applications were granted and 106 were reported as being refused. The National Association of Probation Officers asserted that "there is ample evidence of the issuing of ASBOs by the courts being inconsistent and almost a geographical lottery. There is great concern that people are being jailed following the breach of an ASBO where the original offence was itself non-imprisonable" (Home Affairs, 2005). There is also evidence that ASBOs have been used where people have mental health or substance abuse problems where treatment would have been more appropriate (Campbell, 2002).

Apparently due to the ineffectiveness of ASBOs, new policies were suggested in 2010 by the coalition government to streamline the tools available to tackle anti-social behaviour. This raises questions about the putting into practice of social and justice policies. Barton and Johns (2013) argue that policies implemented "in the real world" differ from their design due to wide discretion accorded to street-level stakeholders, including police officers, court officials and correctional officers. Despite this, other jurisdictions such as from Scotland to South Australia have considered or implemented similar behaviour orders.

There are reports that anti-social behaviour has become embedded in some areas, resulting in significant police resources used in responding to it, having consequences for the way in which minor nuisance behaviours have come to be perceived as necessitating a formal police process (Donoghue, 2013). On the other hand, it has been argued that risk assessment tools can be utilised to structure police responses and used for data collation and information sharing, improving the visibility of those who require support, whether as victims or perpetrators, and broadening access to professional resources. Donoghue further argues that the notion that targeted populations are "acted upon" by "experts" employing risk assessment practices is simplistic, neglecting the multiple nuances of praxis as well as the welfare and protective dimensions of victim risk assessments and especially the rising prominence of victims' lived experiences in discourse. This allows the subversion of the traditional dominance of politics/policy in acting as primary determiners of understanding(s) and accepted knowledge(s) of victimisation, vulnerability and resilience.

As introduced in the previous chapter, the area of youth risk and resilience is somewhat problematic. Massey, Cameron, Ouellettee, and Fine (1998) argued that studies of resilience and risk have tended to be value-laden both in terms of how adversity is defined and how resilience is measured, such that resilience equals conformity and risk equals nonconformity. That is, the outcomes used to assess performance in one context may represent only those characteristics that serve that context. For example, appropriate behaviour and compliance in a classroom setting may be construed as a lack of personal agency and independence in another setting. From a constructionist perspective, the objective status is irrelevant – what matters is the claims people make about "social issues". As Best (2001) argues, the claims-makers' orientation locates the problem's cause and suggests a solution. Claims-makers address different audiences, in order to identify and organise people harmed, educate the public and influence policymakers. While it can be argued that claims do not become social issues until the objective conditions are recognised, equally it can be argued that claims need not have objective conditions and can be based on myths and moral panics.

MORAL PANICS

A condition, episode, person or group of persons emerges to become a threat to societal values; its nature is presented in a stylised and stereotypical fashion by the mass media; the moral barricades are manned by editors, bishops, politicians, and other right-thinking people…sometimes the panic…has serious and long-lasting repercussions and might produce such changes as in legal or social policy or even the way society conceives itself. (Cohen, 1972, p. 9, cited by Burney, 2005)

Key elements of a moral panic are likely to include many of the elements of stereotyping:

* Concern about a deviant behaviour or group that is disproportionate to the threat posed.
* A reaction by others (whether the public or authorities) that is more important and receives more attention than the act itself and its effects.
* The development of moral boundaries between "us" and "them".
* Solidarity being emphasised among "us" by increasing our perception of deviation from our norms by "them".
* The escalation of the perception of risk.

Key players in the development of a moral panic may include the media, public, police and policymakers (Goode & Ben-Yehuda, 2009; St Cyr, 2003).

A moral panic about anti-social behaviour serves several purposes: it allows for the construction of an "other" to exclude, resulting in a perception of social inclusion among those who identify as not belonging to that "other" group; it allows for other stakeholders, such as local authorities or politicians, to be seen to address a community concern, while shifting focus from underlying issues such as poverty or a lack of social cohesion. This is achieved through the imposition of criminal penalties or, in the case of ASBOs, public humiliation and social restrictions, potentially reducing possibilities for pro-social engagement including job opportunities.

> The apparently inexorable growth of welfare surveillance over the families of the working class has arisen from an alignment between the aspirations of the professionals, the political concerns of the authorities, and the social anxieties of the powerful. (Rose, 1999, p. 125)

In this approach to behaviour, the language of risk has "replace[d] need as the core principle of social policy formation and welfare delivery" (Kemshall, 2002, p. 1).

THE RISK FACTOR PARADIGM

The Cambridge study (Farrington, 1995) is a seminal piece of research on the relationship between risk and offending. One hundred and fifty potential risk factors were measured, and of these, 39 were identified as predictive of future offending. In this sense, it could be argued that formal definitions of risk allow agencies to make a case for funding and service provision tied to measurable outcomes.

However, while correlations have been identified, causality is less clear. In addition, the sample was homogenous: entirely male, predominantly white and from one small community. Moreover, the majority of offenders included in the study did not belong to the high-risk group and would not have been predicted. Even one of the key researchers involved in the Cambridge study advocates redistribution of resources rather than intervention to improve behaviour, stating that:

> I have long thought that more might be achieved by giving money to the needy with a minimum of formality than spending money on welfare administration and complex assessments of eligibility. (West, 1982, p. 147)

Reductionism is implicit in the risk factor model. This operates on several levels. For example, at the psychological level, the individual is reduced to sets of psychological traits and cognitive processes. At the social level, the meaning and context of rule-breaking (or criminal offending) is ignored; for example, fighting in the schoolyard that may be in defence of oneself or another is not only normal (both in the statistical sense and in terms of peer group norms) but a necessary part of socialisation and "fitting in" within a particular context. As another example of the risk of erroneous assumptions being made about risk factors: being born to a young (e.g., teenage) mother is considered a significant risk factor. However, recent research in the US found that although maternal age was not mediated by parenting or neighbourhood factors (as has often been assumed) or the child's level of self-control, it was completely mediated by the child's level of exposure to drug-using peers (Barnes & Morris, 2012), suggesting a need for further research.

Risk assessment instruments tend to have high rates of error when applied to individuals. They are population or large group measures, and there are much greater uncertainties associated with individual prediction. To some extent, this limitation is inherent in the statistical method; just because an individual exhibits many of the attributes of a group does not mean he or she has all of them or that those attributes will play out in the anticipated way. Probability will also often be influenced considerably by the presence of one or two key factors, such as heavy alcohol use or involvement in destabilising relationships (National Collaborating Centre for Mental Health, 2010). In addition, many risk factors such as low socioeconomic status, neighbourhood disadvantage, and belonging to certain ethnic groups tend to be clustered together. As a result, individuals may appear to be at high risk due to factors that are beyond their control and are the outcomes of structural inequality and/or stereotyping, raising the possibility of self-fulfilling prophecy alongside victim-blaming. O'Mahony (2009) goes further to argue that the predominance of the risk factor prevention paradigm is an obstacle to a fuller understanding of anti-social behaviour and youth crime and therefore impedes effective responses, due to simplistic and exaggerated claims. These claims obfuscate theoretical and methodological weaknesses, in turn failing to fully consider psychological motivations, personal agency and the socio-cultural context.

Drawing on Beck's (1992) and Giddens' (1999) notions of the risk society, Donoghue (2008) acknowledges that the post-modern prevalence of "risk management" in social policy through the identification of risk factors by experts (also see Kemshall, 2002, 2008) has been criticised for putting the reduction of risk rather than the meeting of need in the position of primacy, such that professional or expert knowledge is "crucial in defining, identifying, quantifying and managing" specific risk factors. However, she rejects this construction of the vital role of experts. As an alternative, she proposes that individuals and groups are able to affect anti-social behaviour policy at both macro- and micro-levels. The extant research finds some evidence of the latter. However, the current author's own research suggests that ways of subverting onerous policies about targeting and measuring are more common than the policy contributions that O'Donoghue suggests. For example, a participant who works with young women explained:

> We're funded to work with girls until they're 18, and lots of them have major issues – substance addiction, sexual abuse, under other people's control … you can't deal with these things overnight … well we're not going to turn a girl away because she had her 18th birthday yesterday, so a lot of the work we do isn't really funded and we have to get a bit creative around that. And it takes a while to get to know them, you can't just immediately sit down and start asking questions and thinking about what boxes [to tick], and some of the really important outcomes don't fit those boxes…I had a girl the other day, when she first came she'd come with her boyfriend and he would do all the talking for her, she'd just sit with her head down, and it just struck me the other day, she came in by herself, had her head up, smiling … a different person. Now what box do you put that in?

In this exemplar, the importance of doing preliminary (and therefore unfunded) work is emphasised, along with difficulties of doing formal assessments. Interviews with staff of relevant government departments have revealed the frustration associated with implementing policies that do not have a sound evidence base or indeed may run counter to evidence but fit with the government of the day's agenda.

A salutary example of differing understandings and priorities between organisations was provided by the current author's meetings with representatives of two NGOs providing services to "at risk" youth, on consecutive days. One lamented the fact that funding was tied to both the level of risk the young people engaged with and the achievement of key performance indicators in the form of achieving positive outcomes (such as moving into training or employment) and the vastly increased burden placed on youth workers to complete tasks related to assessment, monitoring and related administrative duties. He estimated that 60 per cent of workers' time was taken up with these duties rather than doing "the real work that needs to be done" and emphasised the range of problems that resulted from these tasks. These included difficulty in finding the time to work with young people and in engaging them in assessment, low staff morale, high staff turnover and, arguably most concerning, the pressure to engage with young people with a high likelihood of achieving positive outcomes – or conversely, to not engage with young people less likely to achieve positive outcomes, usually the ones most in need. The other person spoke excitedly about having just received a major grant to develop an assessment tool to assess risk and outcomes in their specific client group (what they were at risk of, or indeed whether *they* were at risk or put *others* at risk, or a combination, was not clear). This assessment protocol would likely involve a one-hour assessment when first engaging with a young person, regular monitoring meetings and an outcome assessment. Clearly her intentions were positive, and some level of accountability would seem appropriate (particularly given that both organisations are funded in part by taxes); however, there seemed to be no recognition that the assessment protocol she described would be anything but beneficial for all concerned.

Critics argue that risk is interpreted by professionals as "uniform and unifying" (Donoghue, 2013), resulting in the de-emphasising of structural variables and ignoring personal experience. However, the unproblematic/unproblematised presentation of youths as being "at risk", often with no discussion of what is meant by this term, in itself alerts us to the depth with which the concept is embedded within value and belief systems – so deeply embedded that no explanation is considered necessary (Armstrong, 2004). Yet risk is indefinable without recourse to belief systems and moral codes (Lupton, 1999). Further, though the literature on resilience has identified a range of factors that correlate with healthy functioning in the face of adversity, its predictive power is low. We only know that resilient youth are characterised by qualities that we have come to associate with resilience: a tautology (Ungar, 2004).

Though heightened concern and debate about anti-social behaviour is largely occurring in a context in which crime is declining, real collective and individual concerns exist, especially in deprived communities, which have been increasingly disadvantaged by the free market policies which have dominated in many European and anglophone countries in recent decades. Actual marginalisation has arguably combined with moral panic (Hughes & Follett, 2006).

Anti-social behaviour can be constructed in a number of ways, including as a classic moral panic encouraged by those trading on the politics of fear; as indicative of a social and political crisis emphasised by stereotypes; as real divisions between the included and excluded/marginalised of society; or as the outcome of a growing climate of disorder, as exemplified by Wilson and Kelling's (1982) influential article on "broken window theory": if a broken window is not quickly repaired, other windows will also be broken, creating a sense of public apathy and neglect that attracts criminals. While there is certainly some evidence that neglected public spaces result in less care shown by the public (Cabe Space, n.d., provide a brief literature review and case studies in the UK; Keizer, Lindenberg, & Steg, 2008, provide a US example), the visible signs of decline in a community are likely to be correlated with, rather than causes of, anti-social behaviour, with common underlying factors (or confounding variables) such as poverty and a lack of social cohesion (Burney, 2005). "Broken window theory" has been widely applied in the US – for example, through focusing on arresting people who commit petty but visible crimes – and largely trumpeted as extremely effective in reducing crime. However, where it is applied without addressing "quality of life issues" success is often limited; a key is the development of community partnerships (Anonymous, 2006; for further critique, see Miller, 2001; Wicherts & Bakker, 2014).

Public anti-social behaviour, even at a low level, can be seen as an increased risk of crime, especially in disadvantaged neighbourhoods. Those living in these neighbourhoods are likely to suffer an increased (sense of) powerlessness, exacerbated by marginalisation and generalised distrust, in turn leading to social disorganisation. This perception (which may or may not be appropriate to the scale and seriousness of anti-social behaviour), especially when vocally responded to by other stakeholders such as politicians and the media, legitimates fear and defensiveness. This in turn can lead to a desire to differentiate oneself from the "troublemakers" thereby reaffirming oneself as moral and respectable while constructing an "other", an "out-group". As well established by social psychologists and others, this construction of an out-group while absolving the in-group from any role in problematic behaviour also tends to exaggerate difference between the groups and homogeneity within the groups (e.g., "all of those guys at the park are vandals and should be locked up"), potentially dehumanising groups as just "white trash" (US), bogans (Australasia) and chavs (UK) (Cabe Space, n.d.; Garland, 2001; Goode & Ben-Yehuda, 2009).

Punitiveness is linked to socio-economic security, and as discussed previously (Patterson et al.), increased inequality is linked to social exclusion. In such an environment, the focus shifts to criminal justice, rather than social justice; crime prevention, not poverty prevention. The political discourse shifts to "getting tough on crime", "responsibilisation strategies" and "short sharp shocks", followed by harsher sentencing and possibly the lowering of the age of criminal responsibility. Responsibilisation refers not only to lowering the age at which a young person can be referred to the criminal court but also to penalising families – for example, through reductions in social security payments. Families bear the responsibility for the misdeeds of their young people while also expecting youth to take responsibility at a younger age, while scant attention is paid to structural factors (Squires & Stephens, 2005; Stephen, 2009).

Criminal justice interventions individualise; with minimal opportunity to address collective and accumulating harm in a community, though anti-social behaviour undoubtedly undermines social capital and community cohesion. The focus remains firmly on the individual or at the interpersonal level rather than on community issues and crime prevention is prioritised over poverty pre-vention. Crime and disorder is re-conceptualised as anti-social behaviour in which the context – the rise in exclusion, intolerance and excuses for inequality – is overlooked and behaviour seen as typical of "that kind of person".

This focus on youth perceived to be at risk has the potential to embed stigma. As discussed by the members of the Youth Council Care to Independence Programme (Watts, Kumar, Nicholson, Kumar, & Youth Council Care to Independence Programme, 2006), a key concern of young people "in care" (i.e., under the care of state social services) is stigma, particularly in regard to assumptions about and foregrounding of their personal characters rather than the actual circumstances that lead to their being placed in care.

POWER, CONTROL AND INEQUALITY

Behaviour deemed to be anti-social is often more visible in disadvantaged com-munities, but there are multiple understandings of this, such as: a deliberate political focus on young people's perceived anti-social behaviour; diverting attention from other issues; blaming people for causing problems when they are, in fact, victims themselves; both a response to and a symptom of economic decline and/or increased inequality; response/symptom of economic decline; a weakening of informal social controls due to decreased social cohesion, replaced by punitive formal measures; the increasing social exclusion of marginalised groups; and increased powerlessness in disadvantaged neighbourhoods, exacerbated by marginalisation, generalised distrust and social disorganisation (Burney, 2005; Coleman & Hagell, 2007). Regardless, anti-social behaviour is associated with reduced well-being.

Prilleltensky, Nelson, and Peirson define well-being as "a satisfactory state of affairs, brought about by the acquisition and development of material and psychological resources, participation and self-determination, competence and self-efficacy" (2001, p. 143) and view power and control as opportunities to develop these dimensions of health by social, community and family environments. They note that research confirms the role of control in quality of life and both physical and psychological well-being, for both "problem-free" and disadvantaged peoples, alongside empowerment and self-efficacy. Conversely, those experiencing disempowerment are at risk of developing health and social problems. However, there is little literature that deals explicitly with the effects of powerlessness in young people's lives.

Neglectful and abusive family environments are clearly detrimental to well-being. However, it behoves us to remember that neglect and abuse is often a transgenerational cycle and enacted in negative social environments (see, e.g., Bower-Russa et al., 2001). These negative elements, such as working long hours, may be due to broad social and structural factors beyond parents' control and as such powerlessness may also be transgenerational.

Participation in decision-making and self-determination define our sense of agency and contribute to psychological health and enhance self-esteem and perceptions of self-efficacy and control, which in turn serve as protective factors in times of adversity (Prilleltensky et al., 2001) – for parents and for young people who may be in situations of risk.

High inequality is linked to childhood experiences of bullying, conflict and violence (Wilkinson & Pickett, 2010); further, Wilkinson and Pickett convincingly argue that violence is often a response to disrespect and humiliation, a way of "saving face", partially due to increased status competition and hypersensitivity to shame in hierarchical societies. Along similar lines, Layte (2012) has found that the psychosocial response of individuals to the perception of their place in a hierarchical society (or their "status order") has a direct effect through its impact on stress hormones. The greater the income inequality in the society, the higher the level of status competition and the more likely individuals are to perceive themselves as inferior, leading to anti-social behaviour and physical violence as mediating mechanisms between inequality and health.

CONCLUSION

This chapter opened with a statement about risk and anti-social behaviour as a reflection of public anxieties and policy initiatives designed to alleviate them, rather than risk per se. Crawford takes this further, arguing that the language of risk and regulation has been appropriated to legitimise excessive state interventionism, which may have more to do with demonstrating the government's capacity to be seen to be doing something tangible about public anxieties rather than with meaningful behavioural change. Instead, regulatory goals may be appropriated to erode established justice principles, particularly those of proportionality and due process, and the special protections that have traditionally been afforded to young people. Consequently, new means of control have resulted in more intensive (and punitive) interventions (Crawford, 2009).

Many critics of ASBOs and associated policies and attitudes cite Garland's "criminology of the other": the rejection of crime as a normal event in everyday life "redramatizes it – depicting it in melodramatic terms, viewing it as a catastrophe, framing it in the language of warfare and social defence" (Garland, 2001, p. 184). This appeals to the judgement of the obedient "good citizen", pitting them against the excluded criminological outsider. Burney (2005) has observed that Cohen's analyses are pervasive in contemporary social policy, "driven by the political desire to make people behave". However, Donoghue (2008) argues that a focus on the policies and technologies of control obscures the importance of practice and outcome(s) within the institutions charged with controlling anti-social behaviour. This latter point will be returned to in the final chapter.

Judgements about anti-social behaviour are often based on vague or excessive concerns about risk, resulting in individual or family-based interventions that do not target root causes. Anti-social young people are considered responsible for their actions, yet frequently interventions further embed powerlessness reducing the possibilities for pro-social behaviour.

4

ORDINARY ANTI-SOCIAL BEHAVIOUR: EVERYDAY HASSLES

Low-level anti-social behaviour such as minor property damage, fighting, theft and graffiti are common in early and mid-adolescence with at least one in five adolescents displaying anti-social behaviour at some stage (though this varies markedly by country, likely at least in part due to definitional issues; see, e.g., Hayward & Sharp, 2005; McAtamney & Morgan, 2009). Though there is some variation, the most common types of anti-social behaviours in adolescence were fighting in approximately one-third, theft and property damage (Smart, Vassallo, Sanson, & Dussuyer, 2004). However, although the problematic behaviour engaged in by some young people may be what first comes to mind, "everyday" acts of anti-social behaviour are committed by a variety of people in an array of contexts.

In this chapter, some of the more common forms of anti-social behaviour, such as "nuisance behaviours" (e.g., vandalism), "road rage", sexual aggression and bullying, are examined. Common underlying factors, including parenting practices, alcohol use and the role of social norms, will be explored both at face value and from a critical stance.

In the UK at least, anti-social behaviour is often alcohol-related (Office for National Statistics, 2013). Begging beside cash points, abandoning cars and littering are also common forms (Garrett, 2007). Although anti-social behaviour may often be seen as the preserve of the young, as noted by the British Association of Social Workers, people of all ages have been served ASBOs, often for quite minor nuisance behaviours: an "'87 year-old for being repeatedly sarcastic' and … a sixty-three-year-old peace campaigner was the subject of an ASBO application by police after regular protests at Menwith Hill US military 'listening post' in Yorkshire" (Garrett, 2007, pp. 839–840). Nonetheless, approximately three-quarters of ASBOs are imposed on young people, and the vast majority of research is conducted on young people's anti-social behaviour.

As mentioned previously, parenting style appears to have an important influence on the behaviour of children and young people – and, indeed, potentially throughout life. A key theory of parenting styles was developed by Baumrind (1967) and continues to be widely used. The initial typology described three styles:

Authoritarian: Obedience and respect for authority are highly valued.

Authoritative: Standards and boundaries are enforced, but some negotiation is possible.

Permissive: Minimal controls on children are imposed.

A fourth style was later included:

Uninvolved/neglectful: Parents place their own needs above those of their child (Burton, Westen & Kowalski, 2009).

Further work was contributed by Maccoby, Martin and others (Maccoby & Martin, 1983), though it should be noted that parents may move between styles depending on circumstances. Nonetheless, one style will tend to be more dominant. Key features of the typology are given in Table 4.1.

Table 4.1   Parenting styles typology

Style	Involvement	Control	Independence	Outcome
Authoritative	Responsive, warm, sensitive, attentive	Reasonable demands are made, which are consistent and explained	Parent encourages discussion, joint decision-making; the child makes decisions according to maturity	Enjoyable and positive fulfilling relationship, self-control, cooperative, appropriate self-esteem and maturity
Authoritarian	Rejecting, cold, overcritical	Coercive, use of force, punitive, psychological control, e.g., withdrawal of affection	The parent takes decisions, rarely listens to child's perspective	Anxious, unhappy, poor self-esteem, defensive, hostile, dependent (especially girls), angry, defiant (especially boys)
Permissive	Warm, indulgent or inattentive	Few/no demands	Child makes decisions ahead of maturity	Impulsive, disobedient
Uninvolved/neglectful	Detached/emotionally withdrawn	Few/no demands	Indifferent to child's decision-making/point of view	Anti-social, emotional, poor development

Authoritative parenting "suits" most cultures, particularly those that value individualism, and it appears to result in positive relationships in general (beyond the parent–child relationship) and low rates of anti-social behaviour and delinquency. In the US at least, this holds true regardless of class or race (Pezzella, Thornberry, & Smith, 2015). Across cultures, children/adolescents from authoritative (democratic) homes are more outgoing, assertive and independent, whereas authoritarian homes tend to result in children and young people who either are overly conforming, dependent and submissive, or hostile and defiant. While permissive parenting may result in impulsiveness (linked to anti-social behaviour, as discussed above) and disobedience, it is the uninvolved or neglectful style that is most strongly associated with "problematic" behaviour.

However, the authoritative style is not an adaptive style everywhere and is uncommon in some cultures; for example, developing independence and individualism, underlying assumptions of Baumrind's typology, is not always valued, compared to having a close extended family. Nonetheless, the results of parenting styles are largely universal; that is, even if it is the norm in a specific culture (or family), an authoritarian parenting style will tend to produce young people with poor self-esteem, hostility and a tendency towards defiance. That said, parental affection is predictive of child self-esteem in all cultures – affection and feeling valued can mediate non-authoritative parenting styles, but is less likely to occur if parents are neglectful or authoritarian.

At this point it is important to note that, if taken at face value, the parenting style model can appear to place blame solely on the parents or primary caregiver. Influencing factors such as parental stress, illness, overcommitment and myriad other possibilities are not explicitly covered in the model.

We can also see family norms coming into play, with the potential for the transgenerational transmission of parenting styles – adaptive and maladaptive. According to Bower-Russa et al. (2001), few people maltreated as children view their experiences as abusive. Further, personal experience with a particular form of discipline is associated with a reduced likelihood of viewing that discipline as inappropriate. A history of severe punishment tends to result in failure to consider that punishment to be abusive, and congruent attitudes towards physical punishment as an adult are associated with using punitive disciplinary strategies in one's own parenting. It would appear that when punitive (authoritarian) approaches to parenting are modelled they are considered normal by the child. This seems logical. However, it has often (incorrectly) been assumed that being the victim of abuse will make an individual less likely to abuse their own children.

ALCOHOL AND OTHER DRUG USE

The misuse of alcohol is associated with increased risk of a number of adverse outcomes such as road accidents, injuries and deaths; risky sexual behaviour and victimisation; and specific anti-social behaviours including disorder, fighting and vandalism. Young people in the UK, Australia and New Zealand are frequently assumed to engage in frequent and/or binge-drinking, and the attendant anti-social behaviours, at high levels. Over a third of young New Zealanders engage in binge-drinking, and by the age of 25 more than 20 per cent will have developed a significant alcohol-related problem (Fergusson & Boden, 2011). However, recently released British statistics indicate that the "binge-drinking problem" is not as bad as assumed and is decreasing. The proportion of teetotal young adults (aged 16 to 24) increased by over 40 per cent between 2005 and 2013, with more than 25 per cent saying they do not drink at all, and 2 per cent of young adults were frequent drinkers (defined as drinking on five or more days in the week before the interview) in 2013, a decrease of more than two-thirds since 2005 (Office for National Statistics, 2015). The reasons underlying these decreases are as yet unclear; changing demographics, such as types of migrants, may play a role (Laverty, Robinson, & Holdsworth, 2015). Nonetheless, alcohol use is implicated in anti-social behaviour and appears normative in some groups.

The ingestion of alcohol reduces anxiety, which in turn lowers inhibitions. It can also cause a disruption in the way we process information, impairing the cognitive control of a range of actions including aggression and other forms of anti-social behaviour. While most people do not become aggressive after consuming alcohol, those who are more likely to engage in anti-social behaviour in general are particularly likely to do so when drinking, as they may already have poor anger control and lower levels of empathy (Heinz, Beck, Meyer-Lindenberg, Sterzer, & Heinz, 2011). It would appear that environmental factors interact with genetic variations that affect neurotransmission. This leads to increased brain activity and impaired prefrontal function that, in combination, predispose the individual to both impulsive behaviour, especially aggression, as well as increased alcohol intake. Ongoing alcohol consumption can further impair executive control.

Certainly, alcohol use is associated with a range of negative outcomes. However, the proportion of the population so affected is quite small – the problem of excessive drinking may not be as serious as perceived, and most people who drink alcohol do not become aggressive or engage in anti-social behaviour.

Less research has been conducted on the associations between illicit drug or substance use and anti-social behaviour, and further clarity around some aspects would be useful. Although there are strong links between being both a victim and a perpetrator of anti-social behaviour and illicit substance use, there are many variables to be considered. As different drugs have different effects, obviously some are more likely to be associated with anti-social behaviour than others (leaving aside criminal acts engaged in to procure funds to buy drugs, and the selling of drugs); for example, amphetamines are relatively likely to be associated with violence (McAllister & Makkai, 2003), while a 2004 review found that the available evidence did not strongly support a *causal* relation between cannabis use and psychosocial harm, but neither could the possibility be decisively excluded (Macleod et al., 2004). More recent research conducted in several countries does suggest a link between cannabis use (e.g., Gervilla, Cajal, & Palmer, 2011; Popovici, French, Pacula, Maclean, & Antonaccio, 2014) and/or other drug use (e.g., Nardi, Silvia Mendes da, Bizarro, & Dell'Aglio, 2012) and anti-social behaviour, but it remains unclear whether one causes the other. Moreover, a range of factors at the individual, interpersonal, community and societal levels have been identified which increase an individual's risk of experiencing drug-related anti-social behaviour (Atkinson et al., 2009, provide a useful overview of illicit drug use and violence); it seems logical that the factors that underpin anti-social behaviour also underlie cannabis use, and it remains the case that many people use cannabis (and other drugs) without engaging in behaviour that negatively impacts others. However, public use of illicit drugs might in itself be considered an anti-social behaviour; indeed merely being in a public space supposedly with the intention of making a drug deal may be construed as anti-social behaviour (Blackman & Wilson, 2014), and Sadler reports the observation (both overt and covert) and following of young people by the police to catch them smoking cannabis (Sadler, 2008).

SEXUAL AGGRESSION

Although sexual aggression may not fit within common definitions of anti-social behaviour, sexual harassment is common and something most women experience repeatedly to some extent, though it is rarely quantified. Fileborn (2013) attempted to provide an overview of prevalence of sexual and street harassment from international studies; it would appear that upwards of 80 per cent of women have experienced public and/or stranger harassment. The public nature of some of this harassment (such as catcalls and wolf-whistles) speaks to the normality with which it is perceived by perpetrators – indeed some are actively encouraged by companions. Nonetheless, careful consideration was given to its inclusion in this book; anti-social behaviour, as discussed in the first chapter, is often conceptualised as something that is perpetrated outside interpersonal relationships, and most serious sexual assaults are perpetrated by someone known to the victim. Sexual aggression, but not domestic violence, has been included because it (arguably) appears to have a level of prevalence that domestic violence does not (as discussed further below), especially at the level of *everyday* harassment, and in contrast to serious sexual assault, low-level harassment may be perpetrated by people who fit the more common conceptualisation of anti-social behaviour as outside close relationships. However, in the interests of fairness to survivors, all forms of sexual aggression are included in this section.

Prevalence rates for serious sexual aggression, including rape, sexual assault and other forms of sexual coercion, are often considered somewhat unreliable due to definitional issues and low reporting rates, though this does depend on the source (e.g., crime statistics versus anonymous survey). The WHO reports that globally 7.2 per cent of women reported ever having experienced non-partner sexual violence, with the highest prevalence in the high-income region, consisting of Western Europe, Australasia and Japan (12.6 per cent) and the African region (11.9 per cent), while the lowest prevalence was found for the South-East Asian region (4.9 per cent) (Department of Reproductive Health and Research of the World Health Organization, London School of Hygiene and Tropical Medicine, & Council, 2013). However, excluding intimate partners gives a misleading picture; for example in the US, approximately half of rapes are committed by intimate partners (Centers for Disease Control, 2012); these rapes would not be included in the WHO data.

Data from the "Crime Survey for England and Wales" reveals that, on average during the period 2009–2012, 2.5 per cent of women and 0.4 per cent of men said they had been a victim of a sexual offence (including attempts) in the previous 12 months; one in five women reported being a victim since the age of 16. These experiences span the full spectrum of sexual offences, including rape and sexual assault, to indecent exposure and unwanted touching. Approximately one in 200 women reported being a victim of the most serious offences of rape or sexual assault by penetration in the previous year. Only 15 per cent of victims of these types of offences said they had reported the incident to the police, but even fewer reported less serious offences (Ministry of Justice, 2013).

Approximately one-third of women and 9 per cent of men in New Zealand report having experienced sexual assault in their lifetime. Three-quarters of these assaults against women and 54 per cent of assaults against men were committed by a partner, ex-partner or family member (Mayhew & Reilly, 2009). However, only a small percentage of these are reported to the police, with approximately 40 per cent of those resulting in a conviction (New Zealand Family Violence Clearinghouse, 2014).

Though many of these assaults are carried out in private (with the obvious exception of gang rapes), this may be due to fear of being prevented in the act rather than a sense of wrong-doing per se; in the last few years there have been a number of cases of sexual assault recorded and posted on the Internet as a means of boasting (e.g., the US Steubenville rape case[1] and the New Zealand "Roastbusters"[2] scandal, both of which made headlines across the world). Cole (2006) found that of the 3.5 per cent of female US college students who had been raped, not only did 90 per cent know the rapist, most of the rapes occurred in a social setting such as at a party. This suggests that the behaviour is considered normal among the perpetrators' peers. A further discussion of gang rape will be included in the next chapter.

Although the majority of sexual assaults are perpetrated by someone known to the victim/survivor, fear of sexual assault limits women's full participation in society – for example, by constraining their choices around travel, night-time recreational and work activities – and the consequences of sexual assault are significant.

The study of the role of pornography in legitimising sexual assault or increasing rape myth acceptance has attained new importance with the increased availability of pornography via the Internet and social media. The impact of sexually objectifying music videos is also causing increasing concern. These will be discussed further in Chapter 6.

There are many studies that link aggression and anti-social behaviour among girls and women to a history of sexual abuse (Baglivio & Epps, 2015; Edmond, Auslander, Elze, & Bowland, 2006; Fazel, Singh, Doll, & Grann, 2012; Fergusson, Lynskey, & Horwood, 1996; Flett et al., 2012; Garnefski & Arends, 1998; Holguin & Hansen, 2003; Polier et al., 2010; Polusny & Follette, 1995; Young, 2009) as well as other negative outcomes such as severe depression and self-harm in various forms (Curtis, 2006), in themselves linked to anti-social behaviour.

---

[1] Videos and photographs were taken of a 16-year-old girl who was sexually assaulted over the course of several hours. These were posted during the assault and afterwards on social media, with hundreds of comments made via twitter and text messages – the majority degrading the victim and lauding the actions of the perpetrators.

[2] The Roastbusters case involves a group of young men who allegedly sought to intoxicate underage girls to rape them and subsequently posted video on social media. Friends of the group publicly claimed that the behaviour of the young men was nothing more than "normal teen antics". Despite complaints being made, no charges have been laid.

GENDERED EVERYDAY ANTI-SOCIAL BEHAVIOUR

By middle childhood, children share gender stereotypes and organise information about femininity and masculinity into gender schemas. Although there are
some cultural variations, there are also universal categories, including that boys
and men are (and should be) active, aggressive and dominant, while girls and
women are affectionate, emotional, sensitive and nurturing. In general, there
is a large degree of overlap – some women will exhibit "male" characteristics
and vice versa, and the differences tend to be exaggerated (and erroneously
assumed to be "natural"). Nonetheless, this socialisation of gender impacts
anti-social behaviour.

Despite girls' supposed socialisation to be non-confrontational, research
discusses aggressive and anti-social behaviour in girls. A distinction is often
made between verbal and physical aggression, more commonly associated
with males, and indirect/relational/social aggression, associated with females.
Girls and women's aggression tends to be characterised as more manipula-
tive, cunning, exclusionary and covert: "the perpetrator attempts to inflict
pain in such a manner that he or she makes it seem as though there is no
intent to hurt at all" (Bjorkqvist, cited by Goodwin, 2006). However, girls'
aggression can also be direct, going against gender roles. Some research
(e.g., Moffitt, Fergusson) suggests that girls engage in direct aggression as
much as boys, but it is less likely to be observed or reported. Nonetheless,
fewer girls and women engage in anti-social behaviour, with less frequency
and less severity overall, though possibly violent behaviour is increasing
(Hagell, 2007).

Simmons (2005) argues that among (US) girls, assertiveness is derided and
they are not taught conflict resolution skills, because nice, middle-class girls
do not need them, so they react to problematic situations by covert aggression. Bullying tends to be seen by teachers and parents as a developmental
phase and therefore has tended to be minimised, sometimes with the onus
placed on the victim to learn better social skills. While her work is largely with
middle-class girls, she does suggest that working-class and/or minority girls
may be socialised to use aggression – that it is modelled by others and normalised. Indeed, in situations of economic struggle or other marginalisation,
self-assertion and aggression can be a necessity. Quoting bell hooks, Simmons
says that while assertiveness and honesty may be associated with confidence
and self-esteem, this is not necessarily the case; the outspoken girl may still feel
worthless, but has no option. While women's anti-social behaviour goes against
broad societal norms, it may fit with a sub-culture.

BULLYING

While bullying may be most often associated with the schoolyard, it can, of course, occur in other contexts, and workplace bullying appears to be increasingly common. The use of technology for bullying, especially by children and adolescents, will be discussed in Chapter 6. Due to space constraints, this section will briefly discuss workplace bullying.

Daw, discussing the US situation, reported that more than 50 per cent of workers lost time at work worrying about others' bad behaviour, and 10 per cent of physical violence takes place in work environments. Underlying reasons appear to be boredom, anxiety and stress; 10 per cent consider workplace stress to be a major problem in their lives, with 23 per cent having been driven to tears by it (Daw, 2001). Johnson and Indvik report similar findings, adding that increasing diverse workplaces add to the problem with cultural differences in communication styles, and people who have been treated badly by superiors when subordinates (or by teachers when students) are doing the same when the opportunity arises (Johnson & Indvik, 2001). More recent research found that at least 90 per cent of workers have experienced rudeness or incivility, and a large number report the intention to "get even". Work environments which focus on individual, short-term contributions, such as those who employ large numbers of part-timers, sub-contractors and temporary workers may foster workplace rudeness, presumably due to increased stress arising from uncertainty, and minorities, women and other disenfranchised employees are particularly vulnerable to workplace rudeness (Loi, Loh, & Hine, 2015).

ROAD RAGE

As discussed by Goode and Ben-Yehuda (2009), "road rage" has been considered a "plague", attracting more public concern than drunk-driving, yet it results in very little physical harm. Similarly, there is no shortage of research on road rage, examining links to anger in general, workplace stress (Hoggan & Dollard, 2007), drug and alcohol use (e.g., Fierro, Morales, & Álvarez, 2011) and borderline personality (Sansone, Lam, & Wiederman, 2010), to name a few; there has even been a recommendation that "Road Rage Disorder" be accepted into the DSM (Ayar, 2006). Roberts and Indermaur (2005) conducted an analysis of the extent of road rage stories in the media and compared these results against the incidence of such events reported to the police and survey results on the perceived likelihood of being involved in a road rage incident. Their findings support those of Goode and Ben-Yehuda (2009).

Road rage certainly appears to be common, with at least a third of people in the US admitting to engaging in it (Sansone & Sansone, 2010). However, the vast majority of incidents appear to be at a very low level, with less than 2 per cent resulting in serious damage or injury. A Canadian study found that in the past year nearly half of the drivers were sworn or shouted at or had rude gestures made at them, and 7.2 per cent were threatened with personal injury or damage to their vehicle (Smart, Mann, Zhao, & Stoduto, 2005); however, frequency appeared to be trending downwards.

In contrast, an Australian survey, also published in 2005, suggests that perceived incidents of anti-social driving behaviour are increasing. Of nearly 5,000 drivers surveyed, 44 per cent reported they had gestured or shouted at another driver (of which 82 per cent thought that their response was justified), increasing from 22 per cent in 1996, and 14 per cent reported they had been angry enough to tailgate another driver while flashing their headlights (with 44 per cent believing that their response was justified), up from 5 per cent in 1996. Of those who had experienced road rage by another, 79 per cent had been subjected to rude gestures, 16 per cent had been forced off the road and 4 per cent had been physically attacked by another driver (although it is not immediately clear how many in total had experienced road rage; Hoggan & Dollard, 2007). Hoggan and Dollard also found that individuals who have a tendency to experience intense and frequent anger more generally are also more angry when driving and also link "road rage" to a perceived imbalance between high effort and low reward in the workplace, resulting in general anger, in turn increasing anger in driving situations.

ENVIRONMENTAL DAMAGE

"Environmental damage" (as introduced in the first chapter) refers to vandalism, including graffiti as well as deliberate destruction of other's property, littering and so forth. As noted above, the 2003/4 BCS reported that a quarter of the public perceive this to be a problem in their area (Home Office Development and Practice Report, 2004). It would seem that the anti-social behaviours of most concern to the public then (though only a minority) are acts of environmental damage.

The influential "broken windows theory" (Wilson & Kelling, 1982) was introduced in Chapter 3. To recap, this theory posits that if a broken window (as a symbol of urban neglect) is not quickly repaired, other damage will occur, creating a sense of public apathy and neglect that attracts anti-social behaviour. It has resulted in changes to policing and policy, especially in the US, where the aggressive enforcement of laws against nuisance behaviours has resulted. However, this theory, particularly pertinent to environmental damage, is not unproblematic. For example, Wicherts and Bakker (2014) discuss the results of a study that does not support "broken windows theory" despite using a very similar study design to one that does support it. Miller (2001) suggests that a supposed link between urban neglect and anti-social behaviour, public disorder and other crime is actually the result of other factors such as poverty. No doubt littering is aesthetically displeasing and potentially dangerous, but is indicative of broader problems.

While it seems difficult to find anything positive in other forms of environmental damage, graffiti may include some exceptions. As Baker (2015) discusses, (some) graffiti can be constructed as a way of expressing oneself, and those who create graffiti may be artists or vandals, asserting and challenging notions of citizenship, world renowned graffiti artist Banksy being an obvious case in point.

FACTORS UNDERLYING "EVERYDAY" ANTI-SOCIAL BEHAVIOUR: CONFORMING TO NORMS

A number of well-known social psychology experiments have explored the circumstances in which people conform to perceived norms – even though they may go against personal beliefs or values. Stanley Milgram's work has been mentioned in an earlier chapter; Solomon Asch examined the situations in which people will agree with others giving an incorrect answer – which they know to be incorrect – finding that many people will go along with the incorrect majority at least some of the time but are less likely to do so if another person dissents; when the research participant had an ally, who would also not conform, conformity dropped by almost 80 per cent. It is substantially more difficult to stand alone for one's beliefs than when one is part of even a small minority; any dissent can reduce the normative pressures to conform. While this experiment is narrow in terms of focus and setting and does not consider other influencing factors, it does tell us something about reasons for conforming and types of conformity.

In psychological terms, informational influence refers to the situation where people conform because they come to believe others are correct in their judgements. Normative influence occurs when people conform because they fear the consequences of appearing different from other group members, of not being "one of us". Conformity may be public or private; in the former there is a superficial and external change in behaviour in the public setting only, while in the latter, both the behaviour and underlying beliefs change, and this change is likely to occur in private also; in other words, the new norms are internalised.

While we are all socialised, both explicitly and subtly, to conform to pro-social norms, those norms are context-dependent, and what may appear anti-social may be adaptive or even pro-social if, for example, it gives access to a powerful group, protection or access to other resources. In addition, the norm of reciprocity dictates that we treat others as they have treated us. This expectation may be relatively short-lived, but is powerful in face-to-face situations and leads one to feel obliged to repay acts of kindness, even when unsolicited. An act of "kindness" could be a benefit resulting from an anti-social behaviour, such as an illicit drug, protection from violence or an act of revenge, which would necessitate reciprocity in kind.

CONCLUSION

Anti-social behaviour is often considered the preserve of young men. It is frequently linked to alcohol use, but this and other associations appear to be misunderstood to some extent. Further, the conceptualisation of many acts of "anti-social behaviour" is context- and intent-dependent. Therefore, both the meaning underlying and the impact of anti-social behaviour should be considered. This may be particularly the case with some forms of "ordinary" or "everyday" anti-social behaviour.

What appears to be anti-social to an outsider may be normal to an in-group, and everyday anti-social behaviour may encompass a broad range of acts, from teenagers congregating in a public place to road rage to sexual aggression. In addition, anti-social behaviour may be transmitted intergenerationally, potentially adding a further layer of perceived normality.

5

ANTI-SOCIAL BEHAVIOUR AS A SOCIAL ACTIVITY: GROUP PROCESSES

Group memberships offer many advantages. They help us to accomplish things that cannot be accomplished alone; they offer social status and identity. Group membership usually includes two fundamental types of roles, which can be formal or informal: an instrumental role to help the group achieve its aims, or an expressive role to provide emotional support and maintain morale. Groups also establish norms for members either explicitly or subtly. Whether or not a group is "anti-social" may be open to interpretation to some extent – recall the "problem" of "teenagers hanging around".

Many forms of anti-social behaviour have a social element. While gang activities are an obvious example, there are many others ranging from relatively minor schoolyard bullying to large-scale organised activity, including genocide, at the extreme. Key concepts include situational influences, the development of stereotypes, conformity and the development of "hate-groups". In this chapter, the relevant theories that are applied include diffusion of responsibility and deindividuation and social identity theory to understand how these group behaviours are initiated, explained and maintained.

As noted in Chapter 2, anti-social behaviour often results in, and may also be caused by, rejection by the "normal" peer group. In the case of young people especially, the reinforcement of what is usually considered pro-social behaviour is also likely to be absent in social contexts. Howell and Egley (2005) contend that the aetiology of group anti-social behaviour usually involves a combination of structural deficit, neighbourhood influences, poor school performance and problematic behaviour, ultimately resulting in rejection by pro-social peers. Instead, as individuals associate with others who engage in anti-social behaviour, their own anti-social behaviour may increase for several reasons. Anti-social group membership (1) provides a "training forum" for specific forms of anti-social behaviour; (2) motivation, rationalisation, tools and opportunities for anti-social behaviour are supplied; (3) anti-social behaviour is reinforced by others; (4) anti-social behaviour becomes normal, expected and accepted. Association with this group becomes an important part of the social identity. However, although social psychologists have hardly explored group anti-social behaviour per se, they have explored identity mechanisms, group processes and intergroup relations, in contrast to other branches of the social sciences which have explored gangs and group anti-social behaviour but have generally not included social psychological concepts (Hennigan & Spanovic, 2012). The following section provides an overview of key social psychological theories applicable to group anti-social behaviour.

Crowd psychology, earlier known as mob psychology, is an area of social psychology; key theorists include Le Bon, Freud, Reicher and Tarde. This field relates to the behaviours and cognitive processes of both the individual within the crowd and the crowd as an entity in itself. Crowd behaviour is strongly influenced by the perceived loss or diffusion of individual responsibility – deindividuation (discussed further below) – and the perception of universality of behaviour. Deindividuation and the perception of universality increase with the size and homogeneity of the crowd.

American social psychologist Leon Festinger and colleagues (Festinger, Pepitone, & Newcomb, 1952) first expounded the concept of deindividuation in 1952. Deindividuation is the theory that factors such as perceived anonymity, a sense of group cohesion and physiological arousal can weaken inhibitions and self-restraint in crowd situations, thereby distancing people from their individual identities and self-evaluation in favour of the group identity. The resultant salience of the group over the individual includes a focus on group norms and values. The concept was further refined by Philip Zimbardo (1969), who described why cognitive processes became obscured by the factors mentioned above. It should be noted that deindividuation does not always result in anti-social behaviours; if the social identity one takes on is conceptualised as pro-social, pro-social behaviour will likely result (Johnson & Downing, 1979) and the specific social identity is important (Postmes & Spears, 1998).

As discussed by Goldman and colleagues, gang characteristics readily evoke constructs and processes studied by social psychologists, such as identity and intergroup relations (Goldman, Giles, & Hogg, 2014). It is surprising, therefore, that social psychologists have not contributed more to the analysis of gangs. In particular, relatively little attention has been paid to social identity theory with regard to group anti-social behaviour, though it seems logical that it would play a role, especially with regard to gangs.

SOCIAL IDENTITY THEORY

Humans have a fundamental drive for differentiating themselves from others – recognising the ways in which we are similar to and different from other people. Identity can be conceptualised as having three components: personal, including personal attitudes, skills and preferences; social and group/demographic characteristics such as gender, ethnicity, religious beliefs and particular social groups to which one chooses to belong; and role identities, related to social and family positions and responsibilities.

Social identity theory, developed primarily by Henri Tajfel (Tajfel & Turner, 1979), focuses on the way groups impact on sense of self. Group memberships are an important source of identity, and psychological processes can change in group settings – we may define ourselves according to social identity rather than personal identity, such that in social settings we tend to behave according to which identity is most salient and to perceive others in stereotypical ways according to the groups to which they belong.

According to social identity theory, individuals engage in a three-stage process of social differentiation, which in turn has implications for the development of stereotypes. Social categorisation is the process of deciding which social groups one belongs to. These categories may be based on demographic factors or chosen groups such as "football fan".

Next, social identification occurs: identifying with an in-group more overtly. The norms and values of other group members are seen as compatible with one's own; as we are motivated to maintain positive self-concepts, this may involve identifying with groups we view positively, where possible. Third, we tend to compare our in-groups with out-groups. Because we are motivated to behave in ways that enhance our own self-esteem, we are also motivated to perceive our own groups as better than others, accentuating similarities between group members, accentuating differences across groups and emphasising negative aspects of other groups (Hodgetts et al., 2010). We all belong to several groups, and therefore in social settings a specific group identity becomes salient and we label ourselves and behave according to our perception of this label ("football fan" when at the stadium; "parent" when picking children up from school). These identities change our own and others' view of who we are.

As we have a tendency to behave in ways that enhance our own self-esteem, if we have few individual sources of self-esteem there will be a tendency to look more to the social groups to which we belong. If that is the case, we are motivated to perceive our own groups positively and identify with them strongly. Therefore, in-group members may exert a great deal of influence on each other, and out-groups are perceived negatively, and as very different and therefore having little relevance to or authority over the in-group. One's status relative to others in the in-group also influences group behaviour; we are most motivated to seek to emphasise our commitment to the group and behave negatively towards outsiders when our own in-group status is marginal.

In one of the few pieces of social psychological research into the topic, Hennigan and Spanovic examined intragroup dynamics of a range of peer groups, including gangs. They found that group cohesion and group identification are associated with anti-social behaviour among gang members, but not among members of other groups in the same neighbourhoods. Further, the relationship between gang cohesion and crime and violence was fully mediated by strength of social identity, whereas in other groups, deterrence-related concepts were more important. The authors argue that this difference is due to differing normative expectations; the stronger one's identification with the gang, the stronger the focus on the gang's expectations over and above individual concerns (Hennigan & Spanovic, 2012).

Overall, it would appear that social psychological theories, especially social identity theory, can assist in understanding group anti-social behaviour through the examination of psychological motivations. However, despite common sense understandings and political discussions, what constitutes a group, or a gang, is not straightforward.

DEFINING "GANGS"

There is a lack of clarity about what a gang is and people may engage in anti-social behaviour in a group that does not match the common image of a gang. As discussed by Goldson (2011), Gormally (2015) and others, definitions tend to be too indiscriminatory in trying to capture a complex concept. As a result, people may be labelled as gang members inappropriately (Deuchar, 2010), with the concomitant result of self-fulfilling prophecy, as discussed earlier. Despite inconsistency of usage and meaning, groups are regularly identified and self-identified as gangs.

One distinction that can be relatively readily made is between youth/street gangs and adult gangs, including biker/bikie gangs – though the latter may recruit from the former. The latter tend to be more formalised and structured, while sharing some common features with the former, such as involvement in anti-social behaviour, a hierarchical and sexist structure and a strong social identity. Both also have elements surprisingly similar to the conditions employed in the first phase of Sherif's "robbers' cave" experiments (Sherif et al., 1961): spending a great deal of time together; little interaction with people outside the group; having a group name; and an emblem or other symbolic identifier (whether a gang patch, colour or tag). The result is the strong identification of an in-group and hostility against out-groups.

A key difference between youth or street gangs and adult (especially biker) gangs is access to resources. Biker gangs (or some motorcycle clubs, as they may prefer to be known) usually own property in common (as well as privately), such as their clubhouse or headquarters, for example; these may be fortified (as the law allows) and members are thus able to keep a relatively low profile and enjoy a degree of protection both from rivals and from the authorities. While a substantial income may be derived from crime, it is not unknown for the members to be in well-paid employment. For example, members of a prominent New Zealand bike gang of the 1990s included several self-employed tradespeople and heads of departments of two large industrial companies. Biker gangs also tend to have a particularly hierarchical structure, with the possibility of promotion from "supporter" (a person who associates with the gang on an informal basis and has no privileges) to "prospect" (a prospective member, often expected to be "on call" to perform duties at the clubhouse, such as opening and closing gates for arriving and departing members, "keeping watch" and potentially performing criminal activities, in part to prove loyalty – which will likely also have the effect of strengthening identification and commitment when completed) to full membership once a patching ceremony is completed, in which full gang insignia is received. Once a full member, formal (often quasi-military) ranks may be attained in some clubs, such as "sergeant-at-arms".

It is noteworthy that while gangs may pride themselves on their lawlessness, bike gangs have long referred to themselves as "1%ers": the 1 per cent of the population who are outlaws – in fact the lives of bike gangs are highly constrained by group norms, arguably much more so than the population in general. These norms include the type of vehicle one may own, appropriate clothing, music choices, the expression of emotion (often little emotion may be conveyed, apart from anger) and deference to senior members.

WHY DO PEOPLE BECOME INVOLVED IN ANTI-SOCIAL GROUPS AND GANGS?

Much of the literature describes anti-social groups, and gangs in particular, as a substitute "family" for members, providing a source of support, social connection and solidarity. Political rhetoric in the UK and elsewhere has emphasised the correlation between "problematic" or "troubled" families and gang-related violence. However, the situation is rather more complex than has often been portrayed. In some cases, the gang literally is the family – children have been brought up in a gang environment and the father and possibly older siblings are members. This is likely to result in young people engaging in gang activity as a consequence of family obligations (White, 2009), as well as such behaviour likely having been modelled from a young age and seen to some extent as normal. More broadly, the role of the family as an important factor in encouraging anti-social behaviour, especially within a gang context, is strongly debated. Young and colleagues (2014) argue that the evidence that associates the family with "gang" membership is not conclusive and the precursors to gang formation and anti-social behaviours cannot be simply reduced to poor home environments or "broken" families.

Notwithstanding possibly erroneous assumptions about absence or neglect, a part of the argument about gangs serving as substitute families is the emotional, financial and social support supposedly provided. Moran (2015) examines the notion that gangs provide pride and esprit de corps, concluding that this is emphasised by group processes, including violent expression, and moreover that gang culture provides protection by mitigating potential negative outcomes, such as violence and criminal prosecution, through sub-cultural practices. These may include threats of retribution to rivals and a "code of honour" of refusing to engage with police investigations. The current author's discussions with young women involved in biker gangs have included some parallels. For example, these women, who often do have a history of abuse and/or family dysfunction, discussed the sense of pride, safety and vicarious power derived from members of the public apprehensively watching the gang ride through town with these women riding pillion (the role of women in gangs will be discussed further below). Clearly support is provided, though this may derive from the same source (if the family is part of the gang, as in White's example above).

Though social support and identity are part of the attraction of anti-social groups, they also serve practical purposes. As well as potentially meeting needs for social bonds with peers, esteem and an explicit powerful social identity, membership may provide physical and financial resources. Unsurprisingly, Lachman and colleagues (2013) found that reasons for joining an anti-social group impact upon the behaviours engaged in: those who joined for instrumental purposes exhibited more "delinquent" behaviour (in this US study) than those who joined for social reasons, such as a sense of belonging.

Finally, gang members often (though not always) share the same race or ethnicity, and this identification may be an important part both of the gang composition and culture and rivalry with other gangs.

Therefore, engaging with an anti-social group may serve a number of purposes: psychological, social and practical, and given the broader social context may be both normal and adaptive, especially for young men. However, the position of young women in such groups requires further examination.

Gender in Gangs

Gangs almost always conform strongly to gender stereotypes. For example, most readers will be aware of popular media constructions of male gang members as extremely physically and sexually aggressive. This heavily gendered nature is also usually true of women involved in gangs. Most often, the role of girls or women in gangs is peripheral – they support male boyfriends and partners, perhaps concealing illegal activities, but relatively rarely actively engage in anti-social and especially illegal activities themselves. Their role is normally very subservient and controlled; for example, they are usually not permitted to wear "patches" (reserved for formal members) but will likely be expected to perform menial – and sometimes sexual – tasks for members. For women of low status (not the acknowledged partner of a member), life is likely to require compliance and the risk of what is called in New Zealand "being blocked" or "put on the block" and in the US "pulling a train" – to submit to sexual intercourse with several gang members one after the other. This passive role is particularly common in biker gangs. Women involved in youth and/or street gangs may be more actively involved in anti-social and criminal behaviour, though the gang context is still likely to be heavily patriarchal. However, Morash (2006), writing of the US situation, argues that, at least as far as Latinas are concerned, gang membership provides an avenue of escape from the household duties expected by their families and disrupts some gender norms.

It seems that as well as a distinction between bike gangs and others, a distinction can be drawn between the expectations of girls in mixed-sex gangs and girls in all-girl gangs. The latter are (understandably) less male-centred, more self-reliant and less traditionally feminine, exhibiting, for example, an increased willingness to engage in fighting and other forms of violence – and often enjoying it. In short, the behaviour of girls in gangs tends to exist at either end of a continuum: either intensely controlled and subservient to men, or physically and emotionally strong, eschewing traditional gender roles. Nonetheless, gang-involved girls and women are usually expected to conform to traditional gender norms in some contexts such as when with their family of origin or when they become mothers. Indeed, impending motherhood appears to be a key reason for ceasing or reducing gang involvement (Morash, 2006).

In recent years, female involvement in gang-related anti-social behaviour has gained a high profile. According to these reports, young women are no longer on the periphery of gangs but are important members actively engaging in the acts that are usually considered the domain of male gang members. Young (2009) challenges the dominant stereotype of violent and/or gang-involved girls, including discussion of a moral panic. Drawing on empirical research, she argues that understandings of young women's involvement in gangs should take into account the normalisation of threats and actual violence in their lives; in this context, attempts by young women to create supportive relationships and to exert some control over their lives can be seen as a way to prevent further victimisation, having some parallels to research such as that of Chesney-Lind, Merlo, and Murdoch discussed above (e.g., Chesney-Lind, 1997; Chesney-Lind & Irwin, 2008; Merlo & Chesney-Lind, 2015; Murdoch et al., 2011). Despite currently popular constructions, then, the role of women in gangs largely remains both marginal and marginalised.

"Hate-Groups"

The motivating factors for joining groups in general may be applicable to the joining of a so-called "hate-group" (such as an explicitly racist group). The social reasons for joining other types of anti-social groups are also likely to apply, such as neighbourhood norms, existing family involvement, rejection by pro-social peers and so forth. Membership of "hate-groups" will generally entail several (additional) underlying motivators, such as a desire for "direction"; a need for sense of community; youthful rebellion; existing racist attitudes; a desire for power, possibly bound up with machismo and/or a predisposition for violence; and a perception that the group holds solutions to problems "the reason why there's so much inequality in our society is because x group controls business".

Members are usually recruited through a known person in a gradual process. The initial events that potential new members are involved in are innocuous and the introduction of new norms and thus group socialisation also occurs slowly, until a change to social identity is enacted. Likewise, racist activities escalate slowly, for example, beginning with racist jokes and using euphemistic language to describe aggressive actions and the targeted group (Whitley & Kite, 2006).

Fiske and Rai (2015) make the point that group violence may be socially sanctioned; war is an obvious example. However, the appropriateness of such violence is subject to interpretation, with rationalisations and justifications taking place both during and after the fact. Fiske and Rai give examples including the bombing of Japan in WWII and include chilling discussions of production quotas and points systems for deaths and enemy imprisonments to calculate debits and credits during the Vietnam War. In these situations, not only were (in the latter case, American) soldiers merely "obeying orders" (and depending on the degree to which these were accepted, conforming to norms); in so doing they were behaving morally and virtuously, protecting their fellows and doing their fair share. When taken to extremes, however, dehumanisation results. Dehumanisation can be seen in this quote from Lieutenant Calley, found guilty of murdering 22 civilians at My Lai (Vietnam) and as the officer who issued the orders to open fire, implicated in the deaths of many more:

> We weren't in My Lai to kill human beings, really. We were there to kill ideology that is carried by – I don't know. Pawns. Blobs. Pieces of flesh, and I wasn't in My Lai to destroy intelligent men. I was there to destroy an intangible idea … I did not sit down and think in terms of men, women, and children … I felt then and I still do that I acted as I was directed, and I carried out the order that I was given and I do not feel wrong in doing so. (Calley, 1972, p. 224)

While it may be tempting to dismiss such mass murder and/or hate-crimes as the work of evil psychopaths,[1] this assumption appears questionable. Bandura and colleagues (1996) discuss a number of stages that an individual goes through in order to disengage from her/his morals; most have been mentioned previously, such as diffusion of responsibility and dehumanisation, and Alleyne and colleagues (2014) also use this typology with regard to gang violence, finding that gang members are likely to endorse such "moral disengagement" strategies and dehumanising of victims. However, as discussed by Fiske and Rai, some items on Bandura's scale could be understood as a strong moral engage-ment with one's in-group, rather than moral disengagement, such as:

---

[1] Calley's actions were not seen in this light; he was initially sentenced to life imprisonment with hard labour. Many American citizens and politicians disagreed with both the verdict and the sentence, and it was widely protested. He eventually served three-and-a-half years of house arrest in his military quarters.

- It is alright to fight to protect your friends.
- It is alright to fight when your group's honour is threatened.
- It is alright to lie to keep your friends out of trouble.
- If people are living under bad conditions they cannot be blamed for behaving aggressively (Bandura, Barbaranelli, Caprara, G. V., & Pastorelli, 1996, p. 374).

Once again, the specific context and norms of group membership deserve consideration.

In organised hate-groups, an excessive respect for authority may be involved: a tendency to accept the authorities' definitions and conceptions of problems and solutions. The adoption of nationalistic and/or "better world" ideologies offers hope, although it is often accompanied by identification of an obstacle in the form of an enemy group. Group processes come to dominate as one becomes more deeply embedded in the group, along with being further indoctrinated in ideology and a shared belief system, and one comes to enjoy a powerful social identity. In turn, if necessary, the resocialisation of beliefs, values, norms and standards takes place (Staub, 2003). Potentially the individual learns and changes as a result of his or her own actions (as well as what is modelled): when one first harms another, the victim comes to be devalued more – the perpetrator justifies their thinking in accordance with a "just world" belief system – the harm is deserved. As the harm escalates, so does the devaluing until the other is dehumanised.

Staub argues that group violence is especially likely to be instigated under difficult life conditions, when basic human needs are unmet, for example, because of economic depression, political conflict, decline in a group's power and prestige, and social disorganisation. This results in a need for security, a powerful identity, positive connections to others and control over the events in one's life. If the capacity to control external factors is reduced, psychological needs come to dominate actions. Direct perpetrators of violence and members of such groups have rarely been forced to join a movement that shapes them to become perpetrators. They share the same culture and life problems, so come to share ideas around solutions also (Staub, 2003). From here we can see the underpinnings of terrorism and genocide.

TERRORISM

As is the case with many labels in this book, "terrorism" is somewhat contentious, yet some term is necessary. The common elements suggested by Victoroff appear to suit this purpose; terrorism involves aggression against non-combatants, and any terrorist action is expected to influence a target population and change that population's behaviour so as to serve the interests of the terrorist group, rather than to accomplish a political goal (Victoroff, 2005, p. 4). As mentioned above, despite common assumptions, terrorists do not usually suffer from mental disorders (apart from, in some cases, mood disorders such as depression, anxiety and post-traumatic stress disorder that are common among people living in disadvantaged circumstances, including those in prison) and are not psychopaths. Involvement is usually the result of a gradual process and involves factors such as social identity processes and isolation from other groups. However, Silke (2008) suggests that most of the risk factors for anti-social behaviour do not apply to terrorists. As discussed in Chapter 2, the application of risk factors is not straightforward in any case. For example, Islamic extremists tend to be well-educated and from upper- or middle-class backgrounds, and at the time of joining, most are in professional or skilled employment and married.

In recent years, various studies have examined other factors such as mortality salience, existential fear and different types of worldviews and their association with attitudes to extremism (Pyszczynski et al., 2006); psychic pressure resulting from existential anxiety (Gibbs, 2005); worldviews and "mindset" (attitudes, dispositions, etc.) as the basis of a psychological climate that affects risk of extremism (Borum, 2014); a possible militant-extremist mindset affected by dispositional and situational factors (Saucier, Akers, Shen-Miller, Kneževié, & Stankov, 2009); and the relationship between uncertainty and extremism (Hogg, Kruglanski, & van den Bos, 2013). It is beyond the scope of this book to evaluate these, and it appears that further research is required. Nonetheless, there are some commonalities appearing: existential anxiety, fear and uncertainty triggered by a combination of dispositional and situational factors, alongside a clear repudiation of mental illness as a factor. Much of this research locates "terrorist pathways" or "trajectories" predominantly in the individual; this will be examined further at the end of this section. An additional potential for critique is that the majority of subjects (and this term rather than "participants" has been chosen deliberately) have been men. While terrorists and extremists have usually been men, women appear to be playing an increasingly active role.

Women and Terrorism

Recently, very patriarchal societies may be seen allowing women to engage in one of the most stereotypically male domains – war and terrorism. This activity defies conventional understandings of gender and violent anti-social behaviour (Laster & Erez, 2015). Although women have long been involved in war- or terrorist-related activities, such as disseminating propaganda, spying and carrying ammunition and other supplies to frontline operatives, women in today's conflict-ridden regions are increasingly deployed as active combatants, including suicide bombers. Laster and Erez (2015) contend that women's active participation in terrorism at once defies and exploits stereotypical gender roles. In so doing, the position of women is worsened.

The stereotype of fundamentalist terrorist organisations as ideologically inflexible is called into question by their use of women, and they may be reconsidered as adaptable and pragmatic. Further, terrorist organisations have exploited and subverted gender stereotypes to maximise both the success and impact of their activities. Because women (especially Muslim women in some current conflicts) are often seen as passive and (in some contexts) as victims, they are unlikely to be perceived as dangerous, and especially not as potential terrorists; therefore, they do not attract security attention and appear to be particularly effective, as measured by the number of victims (Laster & Erez, 2015; O'Rourke, 2009). At the same time, they may be considered expendable by men and fulfilling and extending their position as obedient and as caretakers. Conversely, in accordance with Adler's (1975) notion of "deviant expressions of feminism", terrorism may provide a platform to claim liberation from gender stereotypes by taking on the ultimate masculine role. A difficulty to be acknowledged is that outsider perceptions of women's behaviour may be biased, contradictory and simply lacking in understanding; for example, wearing the hijab is seen as an anti-social – even illegal – act in itself in some non-Muslim countries while being considered a symbol of oppression in other countries.

To conclude this section, it is noticeable that much of the recent research on terrorism emphasises psychological factors (sometimes alongside small group dynamics) to provide a scientific basis for assessing vulnerability and risk. This focus accompanies a turn away from the consideration of the political context underlying terrorist acts, in much the same way that, while broader factors may be acknowledged, the "problem" of other forms of anti-social behaviour is laid primarily at the feet of the individual (Coppock & McGovern, 2014). Altheide (2007) argues that the US mass media, in accordance with politicians, promotes terrorism by emphasising fear and uncertainty. Citing extensive media analysis, she posits that messages about terrorism were combined with the established crime-related discourse of fear and expectation that danger and risk are key features of everyday life. This strategic playing on public fears affords the achievement of political goals such as expanding domestic social control and strengthening a role for the US in "defending the free world". Whatever the role of the mass media and politicians in fomenting fear of terrorism, it is certainly the case that few US (or other) civilians are killed or harmed by terrorists (and many more are killed by the police force each year). Nonetheless, terrorist acts are a real problem in modern society causing both psychological and physical harm, and further research is required especially into the prevention of radicalisation.

CONCLUSION

Anti-social behaviour (as defined by mainstream society) often has a strong social element, insofar as it may afford a strong and powerful social identity, social (and other) support and involve conforming to the social norms of a particular group – and being rewarded for doing so. This might especially be appealing to individuals who have been marginalised. Indeed the more marginalised the individual, the greater the length he or she is likely to go to become a member of an in-group. Behaving anti-socially towards an out-group can be an especially effective way of demonstrating commitment and gaining entry to a group. However, it would be incorrect to assume that all members of such groups began from an outsider position.

What constitutes group anti-social behaviour may be obvious in some cases – especially from the standpoint of the outsider. However, constructions of such behaviours are strongly influenced by group norms and beliefs. Further, intentions and meanings may be lost when behaviours are taken out of their historical and social context; acts that are seen as normal and appropriate, even honourable, courageous and righteous, may be viewed with abhorrence in a different time and place. Acts of war and terrorism provide exemplars.

6

NEW TECHNOLOGY, NEW MEDIA: TRANSMITTING NEW ANTI-SOCIAL BEHAVIOUR?

The availability of new media and technology may have increased some forms of anti-social behaviour, such as bullying (particularly due to the ease and anonymity of text and cyber-bullying), provided new means of inciting individual and group behaviours through the use of social media, and increased desensitisation to violence through Internet postings (such as YouTube clips of schoolyard assaults). In addition, the increasing level of violence in entertainment, particularly computer games, and the increase of revenge and Internet porn has become a topic of debate, with links drawn between media violence and increased aggression. As a corollary of the ability to interact with other users, new online communities are formed, with their own norms and moral codes. The evidence for claims and counterclaims about the incidence and resultant harm is reviewed in this chapter, along with appropriate theories and explanations such as habituation and catharsis.

CYBER-BULLYING

Bullying appears to be a topic of some concern and has been discussed above. The perceived rise in cyber-bullying is a particular cause of concern. Cyber-bullying is widely considered to have more severe consequences for victims than traditional bullying. The increase in new technologies such as cell phones and various forms of Internet-based social media has certainly afforded new means of anti-social behaviour, and so-called cyber-bullying has become an issue of considerable public concern, resulting in specific cyber-bullying laws being enacted in a number of jurisdictions including a number of US and Australian states, New Zealand and Canada, while other jurisdictions have bullying or harassment laws that may be applied to cyber-bullying.

Cyber-bullying has been linked to a number of suicides and – no doubt – causes a great deal of unhappiness to many people, especially teenagers. However, the issues are not as clear as may at first appear.

New technologies, especially text messages via cell phones, undoubtedly facilitate bullying; such bullying is omnipresent: it can be carried out at any time of the day, across geographical space and may be done anonymously yet have a wide audience, for example, when it involves the uploading of humiliating material to social media. This contrasts with traditional bullying carried out predominantly over relatively restricted periods of time, largely in the constraints of the schoolyard and with both victim and perpetrator known to each other. Some research suggests that it is common for the victims of cyber-bullying to not know who bullied them (Li, 2004), reducing the possibilities for taking action. Although some studies suggest that girls are more likely to be both victims and perpetrators of cyber-bullying (Carrington & Pereira, 2009; Connell, Schell-Busey, Pearce, & Negro, 2014), this is by no means a universal finding and estimates of prevalence vary, as will be discussed below. The frequency of bullying, unsurprisingly, is a factor in the amount of distress caused, although the variety also seems to have an impact (e.g., face-to-face bullying combined with text and social media postings).

There has been considerable debate in the academic literature on bullying regarding prevalence rates. Because of the rapid development of technologies, prevalence may likewise change rapidly. In addition, different definitions and measures have been used; for example, some studies report prevalence over the previous year, others over the previous three months, and others (though less commonly) lifetime prevalence. Many studies are with high school students, others are with university/college students; it is likely that prevalence varies according to maturity, so these cannot be compared. A systematic review of bullying measurement strategies demonstrated general inconsistency on a range of issues, making comparing prevalence rates between measures difficult (Vivolo-Kantor, Martell, Holland, & Westby, 2014). By way of examples: an online survey of 1,606 new university students in the US found that (1) 35 per cent had cyber-bullied at least one person during their last year of school; and (2) this is lower than traditional bullying, and the authors claim that both of these findings are comparable to the findings of other studies (Roberto, Eden, Savage, Ramos-Salazar, & Deiss, 2014). Another US survey, this of high school students, found that while the prevalence of bullying overall was 55 per cent, 18 per cent of respondents reported cyber-bullying; as no time frame is given, presumably this is lifetime prevalence (Gan et al., 2014). An investigation of 16–19-year-old English students found that 7.9 per cent had been cyber-bullied while a student at that college (West, 2015). Further, young people's conceptions of bullying may differ from researchers.

Baly and Cornell report on a study of 1,283 early-adolescent school students which explored the ability to differentiate bullying from ordinary peer conflict. The results suggest that self-reports are likely to yield inflated prevalence rates as students tended to identify peer conflict as bullying (Baly & Cornell, 2011). Other research in adolescent perceptions of bullying underscores the need to consider their point of view and critically evaluate assumptions. However, regardless of prevalence, the consequences of cyber-bullying require consideration.

According to Wang and colleagues, victims of cyber-bullying reported greater depression than either bullies or the victims of traditional bullying. Cyber-bullying may involve an anonymous perpetrator who distributes humiliating material throughout a large social network, resulting in particular helplessness (Wang, Nansel, & Iannotti, 2011). Sticca and Perren compared the perceptions of 13- and 14-year-olds across several dimensions: traditional versus cyber-bullying; public versus private bullying and the bully's anonymity. The results of the latter two dimensions are unsurprising: public bullying and anonymous bullying were perceived as significantly worse – results similar to that of Wang and colleagues. However, cyber-bullying was perceived as only slightly worse than traditional bullying, with the overall result that the medium per se is less important than publicity of the bullying and anonymity of the offender (Sticca & Perren, 2013). This would appear to suggest that a number of social psychological aspects are implicated, such as damage to self-esteem and the self-concept through public humiliation, and a loss of self-efficacy due to limited or no possibility for control due to the perpetrator's anonymity, as well as potential damage to peer relationships as a result (a loss of friends who do not want to associate with the person thus denigrated, and/or concern that such an association would result in the spread of bullying to others).

A number of empirical papers argue that claims about the "scourge" of cyber-bullying are exaggerated and not supported by the available evidence. Rather, though there are high-profile examples of severe and tragic cases, cyber-bullying appears to be of lower prevalence than is commonly perceived and is used in conjunction with traditional bullying rather than adding to it (Connell et al., 2014; Olweus, 2012; Payne and Hutzell, 2015). Modecki and colleagues identified 80 studies that reported prevalence rates for both traditional and cyber-bullying in adolescents; traditional bullying was twice as common as cyber-bullying, and cyber- and traditional bullying were highly correlated (Modecki, Minchin, Harbaugh, Guerra, & Runions, 2014).

Thus, there is some cause for concern that the focus on cyber-bullying as a *means* of bullying may deflect attention away from the more serious underlying social problems for which young people are *targeted*, reinforcing the marginal-isation of young people most at risk of severe bullying (Cesaroni, Downing, & Alvi, 2012). Cyber-bullying is a socially constructed issue, mediated by attitudes towards young people in general and their use of technology in particular. As Cesaroni and colleagues suggest, cyber-bullying appears to be a fairly "normal" activity – a modern variation on a behaviour that has existed in one form or another throughout history. Accordingly, cyber-bullying is perceived by young people themselves as far less problematic than both academic and media dis-cussions have portrayed. Thus, it is logical for anti-bullying strategies to be aimed at counteracting bullying in general, with a focus on underlying factors in bullies' and victims' lives (especially given that they are often one and the same) and creating respect for diversity.

As noted above, the public concern about cyber-bullying has led to new legislation in some jurisdictions. However, this raises issues about the criminal-isation of young people, with the attendant problems which will be discussed in the next chapter. In addition, frequently those involved are both victims and perpetrators. In many instances, bullying occurs below the age of crimi-nal responsibility in any case (an age at which it is acknowledged that young people are not fully cognisant of the consequences of their actions), so such laws will not be applicable.

In sum, the current focus on cyber-bullying raises a number of issues: a turning of attention away from bullying in general; potential for inappropriate criminalisation; emphasis on the act rather than the underlying factors; a lack of recognition of the significant overlap between bullying and being bullied.

SEXTING AND REVENGE-PORN

Current adolescent use of technology, especially electronic communication, often involves sharing intimate images ("sexting"), usually consensually at the time, but sometimes with an element of coercion and occasionally with abusive consequences. In addition to individual peer-to-peer sharing, images may be forwarded without consent, and at least one of the parties may not be who they portray themselves to be.

At the time of writing, there is discussion in local media which underlines the potential global nature of technology-based anti-social behaviour. A school girl here in New Zealand has recently been blackmailed and bullied by a man in Denmark; the two had formed an online relationship, she agreed to his requests for photographs, and the now common story of requests for more explicit photographs combined with blackmail followed. No doubt this was extremely distressing for the young woman concerned. The story has been headline news, and an Internet safety group has warned of the increase in such incidents, stating that it hears of "5 to 10" similar situations per month. Whether this is a large number for a country of four million people is a matter of personal judgement, but it hardly seems to be an epidemic. A positive corollary of the large amount of media attention may be that young women realise the risks of such behaviour; however, it is likely that those who become victims were already vulnerable, and simply raising awareness is unlikely to be the answer. Young people who engage in sexting tend to experience a range of difficulties, including emotional vulnerabilities (Van Ouytsel, Walrave, Ponnet, & Heirman, 2015).

In the US at least, debates on youth sexting have tended to focus on concerns about the production and possession of child pornography (Mitchell, Finkelhor, Jones, & Wolak, 2012). Elsewhere, the focus is on the risk of exploitation, as in the case above, and the use of images for bullying. As with cyber-bullying, the prevalence is unclear; most prevalence studies appear to have been conducted in the US, and again, specific definitions differ – for example, the transfer of sexually *explicit photographs* via cellular phone (Strassberg, McKinnon, Sustaíta, & Rullo, 2013), or the sending and/or receiving of sexually *suggestive messages* or images (Mitchell et al., 2012) i.e., ranging from transferring sexually explicit photographs only, to the broader sending and receiving of suggestive messages) – as well as methods and samples.

For example, a small anonymous survey found that while more than half of respondents reported sexting as minors, only 28 per cent actually sent photographs (Strohmaier, Murphy, & DeMatteo, 2014); a slightly larger survey of a similar sample – US first-year undergraduates – and time frame also found that close to one-third of the participants had sent a sexually explicit image of himself or herself using a cell phone while a minor (Martinez-Prather & Vandiver, 2014). Adding an additional dimension, Strassberg and colleagues found that while 20 per cent of all participants (US high school students) reported they had *sent* a sexually explicit image of themselves via phone, almost double that number had *received* such an image and of these one-quarter indicated that they had forwarded an image to others (Strassberg et al., 2013). This clearly indicates that images are frequently seen by more than one person, while raising doubts about the accuracy of studies that do not differentiate between sending and receiving sexts. All of the above-mentioned studies, however, have significantly higher rates of engagement than a review of 31 studies conducted by Klettke, Hallford, and Mellor (2014) which found rates of between 10 and 16 per cent in adolescent samples which were either representative or random, but higher rates in other studies (e.g., self-report or convenience samples), and especially when *receiving* sexts was considered – rates of up to 36 per cent (varying by definition). Women are more likely to send sexts, while men are more likely to receive them, and the incidence increases with age, up to a point. The latter point does not fit with the media focus, which is largely on young girls' sexting: the prevalence of sexting increases with age through adolescence into adulthood, with more than half of those aged 18 to 30 years sending sexually suggestive material and a little less than half sending explicit photographs. Over the age of 30 years, sexting rates appear to decline, but this is based on a small number of studies, and the reasons for the decline are unclear. In sum, it appears that the number of adolescents sending explicit *images* has been overestimated; the vast majority (at least 80 per cent) have not done so, though sharing of material is more common as is the sending of suggestive texts.

Aside from the obvious concern about potential exploitation, sexting has been discussed from a number of perspectives, potential criminality (i.e., making and distributing child pornography) being one. Though beyond the scope of this book, as related issues these deserve attention and include potential consequences of shame and guilt, possibly leading to depression, anxiety and suicide (e.g., Ahern & Mechling, 2013); consensual sexting as a legitimate form of expression and media authorship (Hasinoff, 2012) and similar post-feminist views; and the gendered nature of sexting: in recent years, teen girls are increasingly expected to engage in performative sexuality, of which sexting is one form, yet face shame and condemnation when they do so, while boys accumulate status via possessing and exchanging these images (Ringrose, Harvey, Gill, & Livingstone, 2013). The non-consensual distribution of sexual images has predominantly been framed in public debates (often unsympathetically) as a problem of girls' naiveté, resulting in the censuring, blaming and shaming of young women's sexual behaviour, with young men's roles often (though with some exceptions) relatively unexamined (Powell & Henry, 2014).

Revenge-porn typically occurs after the demise of a relationship during which explicit images were provided consensually, when these images are uploaded to public websites in order to humiliate the former partner. It would appear to happen to adult women as well as adolescents and at times includes extortion; several websites have been set up to facilitate the posting of revenge-porn by multiple people unknown to the site administrator, who then contacts the women concerned and requests money in exchange for removing the images. The images are often accompanied by information that identifies the pictured individual and may include links to social media pages, addresses and workplaces. Victims are potentially exposed to both cyber- and physical stalking, as well as difficulties in their employment should their predicament become known to their employer.

The Internet-based revenge-porn phenomenon may have begun with websites that invited men to submit images of their wives and partners in the early 2000s. Some jurisdictions have begun enacting revenge-porn legislation in recent years, and to date, there have been a small number of prosecutions of website creators, notably in the US. If the material concerned involves a minor, child pornography charges may be laid.

While the foregoing material discusses anti-social behaviour that is both technology-based and intended to cause harm, the case of Internet pornography (involving adults) is less clear-cut, even when the people depicted in the material consent to its use.

INTERNET PORNOGRAPHY

Until recently, research into the impact of pornography has had mixed results, with some research suggesting that non-violent pornography has little, if any, negative impact unless certain other conditions are present, such as the passivity of the women depicted (Roskos-Ewoldsen & Roskos-Ewoldsen, 2005). However, much Internet pornography does portray women in passive and/or degrading ways. Recent research has resulted in disturbing findings, such as unwillingness to intervene as a bystander, increased behavioural intent to rape and increased belief in rape myths, among consumers of pornography (Foubert, Brosi, & Bannon, 2011). In addition, exposure to pornography is now routine among children and young people, as discussed by Flood (2009), Owens, Behun, Manning, and Reid (2012), and Fisher and Barak (2001), among others. Increased Internet access has meant that online pornography is now a provider of sex education for young people, with disturbing results. Adolescent boys' use of violent pornography is linked to increased levels of sexually aggressive behaviour, girls feeling inferior to the women viewed in pornography and boys worrying that they are less virile than the men portrayed (Owens et al., 2012). According to Flood, exposure to pornography helps develop and maintain sexist and unhealthy conceptualisations of sex and intimate relationships and increases support for sexual coercion and the likelihood of committing assault among young men. Adolescents who consume Internet pornography are more likely than their peers to have conduct problems, depressive symptoms, decreased social integration and poor bonds to caregivers (Owens et al., 2012) – though the direction of causality is not entirely clear. The long-term impact requires further investigation.

Arguably not pornography per se, but perhaps more pernicious due to its almost complete normalisation is the impact of music videos that sexually objectify women, available not only on television but also watchable at any time on the Internet (and sometimes in more extreme versions). Young men who view such videos appear to endorse stereotypical gender attitudes, greater objectification of women and acceptance of rape (Kistler & Lee, 2009), as well as acceptance of interpersonal violence and adversarial sexual beliefs (Aubrey, Hopper, & Mbure, 2011). "Lad mags" such as Ralph and FHM may be considered especially worrying as they are ubiquitous to the extent of being normalised, yet they often feature strategies for manipulating women and often depict "real women" (as opposed to models) who conform to ideal (and unrealistic, for the majority) body types, are hypersexual and always willing to have sex (Coy, 2009; Coy & Hovarth, 2011).

Music videos and to some extent Internet pornography have become largely normalised; the same can be said of media violence in many of its various forms.

EFFECTS OF MEDIA VIOLENCE

To recap and follow the discussion in Chapter 2 of Bandura's social learning theory, by watching aggressive acts (live, on film or experienced through some other medium), people learn specific aggressive behaviours, develop more positive attitudes about aggression in general and construct aggressive "scripts" – assumptions and schema – with the result that neutral or ambiguous acts on the part of others are more likely to be perceived as aggressive and requiring an aggressive response. As with violent imagery in the music industry, playing violent video games appears to be associated with feelings of hostility and aggressive thoughts.

It may be assumed that interacting with media violence can be cathartic and therefore positive, especially for young men. This argument is frequently applied to contact sports – that an opportunity is provided for young men to "let off steam" and deal with their frustrations on the sports field, and they will be calmer as a result. The same is sometimes said of other forms of supposedly "victim-free" aggression. However, this catharsis hypothesis is incorrect. Certainly, such activities are often pleasurable for those who engage in them and they feel happier afterwards. However, these positive emotions are part of the problem; aggression becomes associated with "feeling good". In addition, aggression becomes normalised and reinforced. At the same time, desensitisation occurs.

Although mediated by other factors, engagement with aggression, whether in "real life" or virtually, influences values and attitudes towards aggression; through habituation one becomes desensitised to violence (when engaged with frequently, it becomes "normal"). That is, a novel stimulus gets one's attention, and if it is interesting, it elicits physiological arousal. But when one gets used to it and it becomes familiar, it ceases to be exciting. Familiarity with violence reduces the arousal response to new violence as one becomes desensitised and therefore more accepting. As a result one may seek physiological arousal through engaging with more extreme material.

Depictions of violence can change values and attitudes through cultivation. In this case, cultivation refers to the social construction of a perceived reality which is inaccurate; for example, the news media may depict the world as more violent than it is, which can make people more fearful and primed for aggression or shift behavioural norms towards increased defensiveness and preparedness for defence or retaliation.

Although the topic of some debate, it seems very likely that playing violent video games may result in increased aggressive thoughts and behaviours (American Psychological Association, 2005; Anderson & Bushman, 2001; DeLisi, Vaughn, Gentile, Anderson, & Shook, 2013); indeed, following their meta-analysis, Anderson and Bushman (2001) argued that the link between playing violent video games and aggression is comparable to the link between smoking and lung cancer.

As with cyber-bullying, violence in Internet fora such as YouTube is a topic that has raised the concern of the general public, for example, home-made clips of school girls fighting. Relatively little research has been conducted on this topic, but it would appear that, again, the level of public concern is not justified, and attention might be better focused on other topics. Weaver, Zelenkauskaite, and Samson (2012) examined violence in 2,520 YouTube videos across three categories: a random selection, most viewed and top-rated, with further comparisons between amateur and professional content. Frequencies and the context of violent acts were compared between these categories and with existing research on television violence. The results showed far more violence on television than YouTube (as a percentage of programming). Additionally, the violence that was present on YouTube showed more context and realistic consequences than television violence.

CONCLUSION

It would appear that public, media and even some academic perceptions of technology-based anti-social behaviour do not match with evidence. On the one hand, while bullying may have devastating effects, there is little evidence to suggest that bullying in general or cyber-bullying specifically has increased significantly and/or has increased harm in recent years. The current level of concern, therefore, may be seen as a moral panic.

On the other hand, with the ready accessibility of Internet pornography, the use of technology to record sexual acts (with or without the knowledge and consent of all parties) and the advent of "revenge-porn", this is an area of increasing and deserving attention. Though largely normalised to the extent that many would not consider usage to be anti-social behaviour, the consequences of engagement with Internet pornography can be particularly pernicious. Further, two particularly prevalent forms of aggression, the sports field and violent video games, appear to attract little public concern and may even be encouraged, but are linked to increased aggression in other settings.

Overall, it appears that new technologies do pose additional risks of harm. However, the focus of concern is largely misdirected.

7

PREVENTION AND INTERVENTION: RISK, RESILIENCE AND RECOVERY

In this final chapter, approaches to prevention, intervention and punishment of anti-social behaviour are discussed, making links to the earlier discussion of politics. While it is not possible to evaluate in depth, an overview of common approaches is provided. The impacts and effectiveness of methods will be compared and contrasted, for example, forms of early prevention and intervention such as diversion, "restorative justice" and "boot camps". Possibilities for dealing specifically with group anti-social behaviour is also overviewed, before concluding with a summary of factors that are associated with success.

Concern about anti-social behaviour has resulted in a substantial body of risk and resilience literature alongside an array of education, policy and practise initiatives that aim (at best) to foster resilience among those deemed to be "at risk" (Bottrell, 2009; Hine et al., 2012; Sanders & Munford, 2007; Ungar, 2012) or to quickly punish undesirable behaviour. As discussed in Chapter 3, the belief that the best way to address anti-social behaviour is through the early identification of "risk factors" has become increasingly common in the Western world (Armstrong, 2003; Bottrell, Armstrong, & France, 2010; Muncie, 2007b). It is largely driven by the belief that this allows for accurate targeting of those most likely to offend (and/ or of their families), thus enabling interventions before an individual's life trajectory is seemingly inevitably aimed towards imprisonment and other negative life outcomes (Armstrong, 2004; McWhirter, McWhirter, McWhirter, & McWhirter, 2013). However, this trust in the identification of risk factors, and the resultant prevention and intervention measures, may be misplaced.

Constructing intervention through the lens of "risk" is likely to be incompatible with the effective engagement of young people who are experiencing difficulties.

Not only does risk become an individualised factor, drawing attention away from social issues and structural inequalities, there are serious issues with some assessment tools (see Bateman, 2011, for a discussion of one commonly used in the UK – "Asset"). The perception of unfair treatment (based on risk assessment) is likely to impair effective relationships and may build resentment, as well as resulting in a self-fulfilling prophecy.

As Briggs (2013) discusses, risk assessment tools have been spliced into a youth work and youth justice environment in which professionals have traditionally exercised discretion and judgement. Assessment tools imposed alongside "key performance indicators" and "national standards" may lead to tensions between complying with contracted outcomes and exercising professional judgement as to appropriate approaches to dealing with young people, as discussed in Chapter 3. This focus on youth deficit has the potential to embed stigma, leading to several negative sequelae, such as reduced self-esteem and self-efficacy – a particular issue for those who already have a background of abuse and the attendant issues of powerlessness. As discussed earlier, the labelling of young people as deviant may have social repercussions, closing off life chances. Such opportunities may already have been minimised by structural inequalities and a lack of social and cultural capital.

Morash (2006) discusses the frequency of a history of abuse in the lives of young women before the courts, noting, for example, that what may be viewed as "oppositional defiance disorder" could (if one wishes to continue pathologising) often be construed as post-traumatic stress disorder. The justice or "welfare" facility itself may also be a site of victimisation. In New Zealand, the Department of Internal Affairs' "Confidential Listening and Assistance Service", set up in 2008 to hear the stories of those abused and neglected while in state care, has heard from more than 1,100 people (many of these cases being historical, in some cases dating back decades). For a country of four million, this appears to be a large number, but is difficult to quantify as further detail such as the number of people who have been in welfare care is not readily available. What is known, however, is that in the year ended 2014, 117 of approximately 5,000 children in care (2.3 per cent) were abused, 39 by their state-approved carer (Children's Commissioner, 2015). Thus, there is a multidimensional engagement with risk for these young people: usually removed from their family home at least in part for their own protection, but also considered to potentially engage in behaviour presenting risk to themselves and others, yet placed in situations of further risk.

At the same time, it would appear that the impact – indeed, in some cases, the stated intent – of interventions for "at risk" youth is to constrain them and limit their choices/power (e.g., choice of friends). This is borne out by the literature's preoccupation with "chaotic" families and communities (Chichetti, Toth, & Rogosch, 2000; Wyman, Sandler, Wolchik, & Nelson, 2000) with the implication that control is lacking, echoed by the arguments above in regard to a perceived moral panic and media calls for "boot camps" and harsher (particularly custodial) penalties for youth offenders.

When powerlessness or related issues are discussed with regard to risk and justice, it is usually in terms of individual psychological states such as reduced coping, self-esteem, anxiety and depression, with the corollary that the onus is on the individual to overcome these states; the socio-political realities that underpin risk are frequently ignored. As discussed by Cox (2012), the process of desistance may be tied to the individuals' sense of the appropriateness of penalties or mandated interventions. When a young person enters a programme or intervention with a sense of powerlessness or pessimism about the fairness of the process, they are unlikely to fully engage with the programme. This sense of unfairness may also result in resistance due to a sense of injustice.

PREVENTING ANTI-SOCIAL BEHAVIOUR

Prevention programmes are generally aimed at those "at risk" (a problematic term in itself), but it may be possible to reduce the need for those programmes on an interpersonal level. Depending on individual circumstances, caregivers, teachers and other adults in a young person's life may be able to encourage and reward good behaviour; focus on the child's strengths, thereby building self-esteem; engage the child in enjoyable activities. If punishment is considered necessary, it should be focused on the loss of privileges while ensuring the reason for punishment is understood and is not seen as merely a demonstration of anger or strength.

Key Characteristics of Effective Prevention Programmes

Of those aimed at individual young people, interventions that embody therapeutic philosophies aimed at supporting positive change are the most successful overall. Training which aims to teach young people social and emotional competence by addressing appropriate problem-solving, communication and anger management skills seems most effective. These contrast with programmes based on strategies of coercion or control, such as surveillance and discipline. These are far less effective and may actually make matters worse in some cases, as discussed above. The quality of programme implementation is important to the extent that a less effective but well-implemented programme is likely to outperform a more effective programme that has been poorly implemented (see Case & Haines, 2014, for an example of a programme that prioritises inclusionary, participatory and legitimate practices, and Ross, Duckworth, Smith, Wyness, & Schoon, 2010, for a review of international literature).

Mentoring programmes appear to have grown in popularity in recent decades. Such programmes typically involve a non-professional drawn from the community spending time with an "at risk" young person in a supportive capacity while also acting as a role model. Farruggia, Bullen, Dunphy, Solomon, and Collins (2010) conducted a review of 23 active mentoring programmes operating in New Zealand; however, only 35 per cent had conducted evaluations examining their effectiveness. Programmes that focused on psychological and interpersonal goals were more effective than programmes that focused on educational, behavioural, vocational or cultural goals. There were many factors that appeared to moderate effectiveness such as the type of mentoring relationship, the level of structure, use of peers as mentors, expected length of mentor–mentee relationship, socio-economic status of youth, and researcher–practitioner relationship. However, they note that although 88 per cent of the programmes included in their review showed some level of effectiveness, the results are tentative due to the varied quality of the primary evaluations.

Taheri and Welsh (2015) conducted a review of studies of 17 afterschool programmes, primarily from the US, including academic, recreation and skills training and/or mentoring. The programmes overall had some benefits, but not at a statistically significant level. Although nothing suggested that any of the programmes should be discontinued, neither were any particularly well-supported. It does appear that such programmes are more effective when structured and well-supervised.

Effective school-based programmes tend to be aimed at changing the school environment rather than changing the young person alone. These programmes include interventions that emphasise interactive instructional methods using cognitive behavioural techniques; grouping together anti-social pupils for parts of the day; discipline and management strategies that draw on staff and members of the community to enhance school capacity and evaluate structures.

Within family-focused prevention, behavioural parent training and multi-systemic therapy seem particularly effective. Behavioural parent training teaches parents to be consistent in reinforcing positive or desirable behaviour and ignoring or punishing uncooperative or anti-social behaviour. Multi-systemic therapy is an intensive, personalised, home-based therapeutic intervention, usually targeted at high-risk young people. Depending on individual needs, this could include skills training in the young person, parenting skills, measures aimed at decreasing a young person's association with anti-social peers and measures for improving academic engagement.

INTERVENTIONS

Along with rational choice theory, the "responsibilisation" of young people is a concept that has increasingly informed youth justice policy internationally. However, there is little evidence that such approaches are effective. Additionally, policy in many jurisdictions focuses not on supporting desistance but on containment and behaviour modification. These strategies anticipate "rational" thinking in young people, rather than delivering justice (Barry, 2013). As with most of the prevention programmes mentioned above, many aimed at reducing anti-social behaviour, have either not been subject to rigorous evaluation (Berry, Little, Axford, & Cusick, 2009) or have only limited support (if any). Nevertheless, this section overviews common intervention strategies, including restorative justice, diversion, ASBOs, psychological interventions (with a brief discussion of the developing possibilities of neuroscience), boot camps, and imprisonment.

Restorative Justice

In contrast to the primarily punitive approaches of ASBOs, boot camps and imprisonment (which will be discussed below), restorative justice includes rehabilitative and social amelioration components. Restorative justice is a process whereby (ideally) all stakeholders meet with the aim of collectively resolving how to deal with the aftermath of a criminal offence. By this definition it is clearly not appropriate for all forms of anti-social behaviour, but is frequently used in cases of youth offending. There is potential for all parties to come to understand the experiences of others and implications for the future, and thereby meet the needs of both victim and offender. The retributive nature of most traditional justice systems is replaced by a focus on repairing violations (Haines & O'Mahony, 2006). As discussed by Wood (2015), the goals of restorative justice may be articulated on macro-, meso- and micro-levels. Macro-level goals focus on the transformation of criminal justice practices and policies that may reduce imprisonment, as well as other practices designed to degrade or shame offenders. Meso-level goals include community involvement in restorative practices that may contribute to the ability of communities to reduce crime and improve quality of life. As noted above, micro-level goals are oriented towards providing an opportunity for exchanging views, ameliorating harm to victims and offender accountability and reparations.

However, the practise of restorative justice differs markedly. For example, some jurisdictions including New Zealand and Northern Ireland take a "youth conference" approach, with the onus on the offender reflecting on their offending, often resulting in an apology to the victim and the development of a restoration plan. Thus, this form of restorative justice has the potential to address the past, present and future, in contrast to the focus on the past of punitive/retributive approaches (Walgrave, 1995). Further, with the victim and their needs being central, theoretically, restorative justice should achieve a positive outcome for all stakeholders, including the victim. However, the ultimate efficacy of restorative justice has been questioned.

Although restorative justice has often been embraced enthusiastically, debate about its definition, practise and appropriateness continues. As discussed above, explicitly punitive approaches are rarely effective and may be counterproductive, increasing undesirable behaviour; clearly, this does not fit with the principles of restorative justice as it is usually conceptualised. However, the involvement of a range of stakeholders invites the possibility that retribution will be sought, at least by the victim and possibly by others. Depending on the form that the practise takes and other factors such as the orientation and skills of the facilitator, a wish for retribution may be averted; however, this may reduce the restorative aspect for the victim. On the other hand, the punishment that the victim may desire reduces restoration and long-term positive outcomes for the victim (and more broadly). A further issue is the obligation for reciprocity. An aim of a restorative justice, as mentioned above, may be for the offender to apologise to the victim. In many cultures, depending on the seriousness of the offending, this norm of reciprocity would result in internal (and possibly external) pressure for the victim to accept the apology and absolve the offender, regardless of any negative residual feelings. Gal and Moyal (2011) report that dissatisfaction with the process can result in serious harm for victims. Reviewing a number of studies in several countries, Wood (2015) identifies additional issues. These include limited evidence for a reduction in imprisonment or even reoffending; insufficient attention to the drivers of crime; attempting to address macro-social problems with a micro-social solution.

Diversion

"[U]nless the public interest requires otherwise, criminal proceedings should not be instituted against a … young person if there is an alternative means of dealing with the matter", so states the New Zealand Children, Young People and their Families Act (1989), recognising that contact with the formal criminal justice system can be detrimental. A significant minority of boys and young men will commit minor crimes; in particular, a substantial number are committed by 12- and 13-year-olds, but are very minor. Although the shock of a formal process at an early stage might be expected to deter young people from reoffending, it often has the opposite effect; contact with the formal justice system increases the likelihood of increasing the level of criminal activity in early adulthood.

Bringing the young person before the court has at least four consequences that have the potential to encourage a young person's self-identification as an offender: increased vulnerability to peer contagion; desensitisation to the criminal justice system; the self-fulfilling effect of the "offender" label; and the court appearance as a badge of honour, earning respect from anti-social peers. Alternatives may include a formal caution, attendance at a family group conference or restorative justice process.

Diversion from the criminal justice system is an example of a welfare approach, in keeping with the UN Convention on the Rights of the Child: "the desirability of promoting the child's reintegration and ... constructive role in society". Moreover, young people referred to diversion generally have significantly lower rates of reoffending (see, e.g., McAra & McVie, 2010; Wilson & Hoge, 2013), though Richards (2014) raises some issues about rationales, objectives and practice and, in particular, its individualistic nature that ignores social determinants of crime.

"Aging Out" and Desistance

Many studies show that punitive approaches such as youth imprisonment dramatically increase the likelihood of ongoing offending; this will be discussed further below. In contrast, as many as a third of young people will engage in anti-social behaviour (depending on the definition) before they grow up but will naturally "age out" of this behaviour as they mature. While this rate of anti-social behaviour may seem high, the desistance rate is equally high; most young people will desist without formal intervention. For those who have more trouble, establishing a relationship with a significant other (a partner or mentor) and employment correlate with young people aging out of anti-social behaviour as they reach adulthood (Holman & Zeidenburg, 2006). This desistance may also contain elements of self-control (Gottfredson & Hirschi, 1990) and Moffitt's adolescence-limited developmental theory (1993, 2006), both included in Chapter 2.

Psychological Interventions

A recent review of treatment for conduct disorder found that, although often conceptualised as an illness affecting an individual, the common theme underlying effective interventions is change in the environment around the young person, for example, via parent training rather than psychological treatment, while medication is shown to be largely ineffective (Scott, 2008).

Similarly, a systematic examination of the evidence for the effectiveness of psychological treatments for anti-social personality disorder found insufficient evidence for any specific psychological intervention (Gibbon, Duggan, Stoffers, Huband, Völlm, Ferrite, Lieb, 2010). Few of the included studies examined key outcomes: aggression reduction, reconviction rates, global functioning, social functioning and adverse effects. Three interventions – contingency management with standard maintenance; cognitive behavioural therapy with standard maintenance; and a "Driving While Intoxicated programme" with imprisonment – appeared to be effective, in terms of a fairly minimal measure: at least one outcome in at least one study. However, each of these interventions had been originally developed for people with substance misuse problems, and improvements were mainly confined to substance misuse-related outcomes. None of the studies reported significant change in any specific anti-social behaviour. Thus, it would appear that the search for effective interventions should be expanded beyond psychological treatment.

Neuroscience is rapidly increasing comprehension of the human brain and has potential applications to justice policy and prevention strategies. In the US, findings from this field have been used as a liberalising tool, given that they demonstrate evidence that young people's cognitive development takes place over a longer period than had previously been thought. The appeal of these studies in some other countries is foreseeable, given how they fit with arguments in support of raising the age of criminal responsibility, along with policies of diversion and the reduction of prison sentences. However, the dual-use dilemma must be considered: while neuroscience can nurture human potential, it may also constrain it, for example, to "prove" poor parenting and "predict" future criminality (Walsh, 2011).

ASBO

According to recent UK lawmaking, anti-social behaviour management in general and the ASBO in particular are pertinent for a number of reasons. These issues relate to the "risk preventive" perspective on crime and disorder management and have a central concern with what Squires and Stephen (2010) call "precautionary criminalisation".

The ASBO is undoubtedly the most significant new order to be introduced in the UK, in part because of its power (including criminal sanctions if breached), but also due to the ways in which the social and political construction of anti-social behaviour has been developed with regard to normalized standards of behaviour. Subsequently, the renewed political and media focus upon anti-social behaviour has seen the act of being "anti-social" now habitually and customarily discussed in terms of both criminal and sub-criminal behaviour (Donoghue, 2008). Although the British government has proposed to replace the ASBO, its replacement would retain many of the ASBO's more controversial features. Cornford (2012) argues that the ASBO and similar legislation is objectionable because it makes criminalisation contingent upon the judgements of victims, and any preventive benefits come at a high cost to autonomy and liberty.

Hodgkinson and Tilley (2011) argue that police and local authorities have been encouraged to see the ASBO, along with a range of other enforcement options, as a panacea for tackling anti-social behaviour and especially perceptions of youth disorder. Hodgkinson and Tilley suggest that rather than abandoning the ASBO completely, it may be possible to rehabilitate it within the context of a range of more pro-active and far-sighted community-based measures. They suggest that targeting the individual or anti-social families does have merit, but addressing the underlying causes of anti-social behaviour in a community is also important and may encourage community cohesion and social capital.

Given the evidence that programmes aimed at fostering positive change are more effective than those based on control, coercion and surveillance, the lack of efficacy discussed earlier is unsurprising. The same appears true of so-called "boot camps".

Boot Camps

Boot camps have been used predominantly in the US, though have gained wider popularity recently. These camps were initially intended for the treatment of adult offenders in response to the growing prison population; it was believed that this alternative "short, sharp, shock" detention would cost less than imprisonment and deter offenders from future criminal activity, consequently reducing the prison population (Jolliffe et al., 2013). There are few research findings in favour of boot camps in light of any of the initial intentions; for example, recidivism rates in the US among former prison inmates and boot camp participants are approximately the same. Although some proponents acknowledge the ineffectiveness of boot camps in reducing recidivism, they argue that this is a small price to pay when one considers the ability of such facilities to reduce the prison population, consequently saving costs. Opponents argue that the military philosophy embedded in traditional correctional boot camps is ineffective, and contradicts the main outcome – to instil self-control, self-esteem and self-responsibility. Critics add that the emphasis on authority is likely to result in resentment, anger and poor self-esteem – not conducive to rehabilitation.

Imprisonment

There are many studies that show that youth detention or imprisonment dramatically increases the likelihood of ongoing offending. In their 2006 report on the impact of incarcerating youth, citing a number of studies conducted in the US, Holman and Ziedenberg explain that confining young people together likely causes them to have a higher recidivism rate and poorer outcomes than youth who are not clustered and categorised together in such a way. This is referred to as "peer deviancy training" and results in statistically significant higher levels of substance abuse, school difficulties, violence and adjustment difficulties in adulthood. It was found that the unintended consequences of grouping at-risk youth may include negative changes in attitudes towards anti-social behaviour and increased affiliation with anti-social peers, and even when controlling for prior offences, they are more likely than non-detained youth to go "deeper" into the system: detained youth are three times more likely to be committed to a justice facility than similar youth who are not detained (Holman & Zeidenburg, 2006).

In addition, detention has a profoundly negative impact on young people's mental and physical health and their future education and employment, in turn making a productive life harder to achieve. Holman and Ziedenberg discuss the finding that at least one-third of imprisoned youth are diagnosable with depression and that poor mental health combined with the conditions of detainment make it more likely that they will engage in suicide and self-harm. Similar results are found elsewhere; a review encompassing 12 countries (Fazel & Danesh, 2002) found that prisoners were several times more likely than the general population to have psychosis and major depression (and, unsurprisingly, anti-social personality disorder); New Zealand research suggests that as many as one-quarter of prison inmates have serious and undiagnosed mental health problems (OAG, 2008). Post-traumatic stress disorder is especially common among women prisoners (Brazil, Matheson, Doherty, & Forrester, 2015; Murdoch et al., 2010), often accompanied by substance abuse; few receive adequate treatment.

In addition to a lack of efficacy at the individual level, imprisonment does not impact structural factors that underlie anti-social and criminal behaviour. As discussed by Greenberg and West (2001), imprisonment rates in the US are correlated with multiple factors including ethnicity, welfare provision and socio-economic disadvantage. They suggest that racial stereotyping of black people leads to increased threat perception, managed within a punitive justice system. This may well be the case; however, the combination (identified by Greenberg and West) of (1) good and increasing financial resources, (2) low welfare provision and

(3) a typically socio-economically disadvantaged group suggests high levels of inequality. Similar patterns are seen elsewhere, as noted previously; some ethnic groups are far more likely to be imprisoned than others and this may be tied to issues of discrimination, class, poverty and inequality.

DEALING WITH GROUP ANTI-SOCIAL BEHAVIOUR

To a large extent, the interventions discussed above are also appropriate to individuals involved in group anti-social behaviour, especially gangs (notwithstanding the definitional issues discussed elsewhere). Nonetheless, there are some approaches specifically applicable to groups. This section discusses gang desistance, and the prevention of radicalisation may result in involvement in other forms of group anti-social behaviour such as terrorism.

Gang Desistance

Gormally's research on gang desistance in Glasgow has some parallels with concepts discussed previously, including "aging out" and social identity, as well as social exchange theory (Homans, 1961). Engagement with a youth gang (or other anti-social group) may be seen as an investment (Gormally, 2015); in common with most relationships and group memberships, gangs offer opportunities but extract costs. As a young person matures, there may come a time when the costs (such as justice system interventions, time commitments, being on the receiving end of violence) outweigh opportunities (crime proceeds, reputation). The individual may recognise that there are other potentially more satisfying opportunities, and their salient identity may change from "gang member" to "father", for example. However, strategies such as those expounded in the 2011 Ending Gang and Youth Violence report (HM Government, 2011) tend to construct gangs and the individuals within them as the enemy, obscuring the wider social and structural roots of youth anti-social behaviour. This focus on gang membership may be counterproductive, criminalising innocent young people at the periphery and creating self-fulfilling prophecies rather than focusing resources on serious violent crime (Cottrell-Boyce, 2013).

Preventing Radicalisation

Recent research suggests that empowering the individual while strengthening empathy may counter violent radicalisation (Feddes, Mann, & Doosje, 2015). Resilience training with a group described as "possibly vulnerable to radicalisation" (p. 408) increased agency – a sense of which is often lacking in people who engage in any form of anti-social behaviour – along with self-esteem and empathy. This resilience training included practical assistance such as support in finding employment, reflecting on acceptable behaviour and dealing with conflicts. The risk of violent radicalisation was reduced as violent intentions decreased along with ideology-based violence. Surprisingly, taking on the perspective of the "other" may increase radical attitudes; it would appear that further research would be beneficial. At the same time, there are clear limitations in the available literature around prevention. Although there has certainly been an upswing in research into the minds and motivations of terrorists, these have an individual focus and thus limited avenues for applicability. This research offers little by way of approaches to prevention and intervention; the individualistic nature requires accurate targeting of "at risk" people (with all the issues discussed elsewhere); presumably they can only be applied domestically, and there is a failure to take into account factors beyond the individual.

What Works?

To summarise, many of the approaches in place have only a limited evidence base – in some, but not all, cases, this is because of the lack of robust evaluation and differing implementation practices such that results differ. However, it is possible to discuss efficacy in general terms. The programmes that are the most effective tend to have the following attributes:

- Clear structure and focus (e.g., in after-school programmes).
- A positive peer culture that encourages young people to promote pro-social attitudes.
- Builds self-esteem and positive social identity.
- Modelling of pro-social behaviour by well-trained staff.
- Clear communication of expectations of behaviour, possibly including behaviour contracts, and behaviour modification methods such as cognitive behavioural therapy.
- Rewards for pro-social behaviour.
- Provision of support to the family (which may take many forms such as parenting training, assistance with employment seeking).
- Drug rehabilitation.
- Attendance to mental health issues.

Conspicuous by their absence are programmes that have the addressing of broader social issues as a significant component. However, addressing social injustice is a necessary prerequisite to tackle the origins of youth offending (Corr, 2014). Though more than 20 years old, most elements of Ritchie and

Ritchie's programme for the reduction of violence are relevant to the reduction of anti-social behaviour, including at the societal and cultural levels (Ritchie & Ritchie, 1993). These include, for example, increased family support, the reduction of violence in media, prison reform and a focus on rehabilitation over retribution. Further, the circumstances of young people defined as "at risk of offending" are often the same as those of young people "in need". As discussed by Haydon (2014), in situations where individual interventions are appropriate, if young people are considered "troubled" rather than "in trouble", the focus could be shifted away from deficits, surveillance and criminalisation to strengths, development and well-being.

CONCLUSION

In conclusion to this chapter specifically, prevention and intervention measures are less likely to produce positive outcomes if they focus primarily on internal processes and dispositions, failing to consider the social realities of those who engage in anti-social behaviour. Further, the current criminal justice systems of many countries do not deliver social justice. Internationally, the justice system has become increasingly punitive in accordance with public desires and misperceptions, and significant racial disparities have existed for some time. For example, Graham (2010) discusses the UK context, concluding that the over-representation of young people from specific ethnic minorities is in part due to direct and indirect discrimination in the justice system. This is accompanied by lower life chances such as a relative lack of secure employment, increasing the potential for transgenerational transmission of anti-social behaviour (e.g., Rutter, 2010).

Second, interventions are less effective if they are purely criminogenic: the promotion of positive behaviour is at least as important as the reduction of anti-social behaviour. Further, punishment alone is not enough – deterrent sentencing does not live up to its name (Muncie, 2007a). Shocking "at risk" youth into changing their attitudes and behaviours by exposing them to already hardened adult criminals and giving them the opportunity to spend nights in prison also have had poor results. Boot camps are the best of these punitive style programmes, but only in that they prove similarly effective to simple probation (McLaren, 2000).

The risk factor paradigm, while potentially useful for identifying groups of people in need of support, is not a safe tool for targeting individuals who may engage in anti-social behaviour. Law and order is increasingly a key political platform in Western politics, with public concern arising from concerns regarding both local and global security. These global security concerns have arguably been emphasised to shift attention away from macro-social local community issues. However, in order to deliver justice in an efficacious manner, several key factors should be considered: anti-social behaviour is associated not only with individual vulnerabilities but also social adversity and structural issues; early identification of at-risk young people is not fool-proof and risks stigmatising and creating self-fulfilling prophecies; harsh punishment is rarely effective.

More broadly, anti-social behaviour in general and some specific forms of anti-social behaviour are not the social issue they are portrayed to be. With the exception of vandalism, most acts of anti-social behaviour impact few people outside the peer group. For example, most people harmed by gang members are other gang members, not members of the public, and many times more people are killed in road traffic accidents than by terrorists.

Not only do incorrect assumptions and the resulting policies and interventions run the risk of being at best ineffective and at worst harmful to the people at whom they are targeted, this obfuscation detracts from the possibilities of providing effective interventions for issues that are having negative impacts on communities.

With regard to precursors to anti-social behaviour, there are a number of factors that have received insufficient attention in some of the literature, and especially with regard to prevention and intervention approaches. The issues with risk factor-based targeting have been discussed extensively above, as have the lack of consideration of structural problems.

Many early theories, as discussed in Chapter 2, remain relevant. Although social identity has received some attention recently, especially with regard to gangs or other anti-social groups, this aspect of anti-social behaviour both as a precursor and implications for prevention deserves increased focus. I would add that insufficient attention has been paid to the "normality" of anti-social behaviour.

The importance of norms has been underrecognised; anti-social behaviour is often normal – both in the everyday sense of the word and in the statistical sense – and as such is often a necessary part of peer relationships and is therefore socially adaptive, at least in a specific context. For prevention and intervention to be effective, this social normality must be taken into consideration. Prevention strategies will be most effective if they are part of a system targeted at the interpersonal, community and societal levels.

Anti-social behaviour does not occur in a vacuum, but is a consequence of the social milieu of the individual. To prevent and intervene in anti-social behaviour, we must understand the precursors beyond those immediately obvious and question our own assumptions and biases.

REFERENCES

Adler, F. (1975). *Sisters in crime.* New York, NY: McGraw-Hill.

Ahern, N. R., & Mechling, B. (2013). Sexting: Serious problems for youth. *Journal of Psychosocial Nursing and Mental Health Services, 51*(7), 22. doi:10.3928/02793695-20130503-02

Alleyne, E., Fernandes, I., & Pritchard, E. (2014). Denying humanness to victims: How gang members justify violent behavior. *Group Processes & Intergroup Relations, 17,* 750–762. doi:10.1177/1368430214536064

Altheide, D. L. (2007). The mass media and terrorism. *Discourse & Communication, 1*(3), 287–308. doi:10.1177/1750481307079207

American Psychiatric Association. (2013). *Diagnostic and statistical manual of mental disorders* (5th ed.). Arlington, VA: American Psychiatric Publishing.

American Psychological Association. (2005). *Resolution on violence in video games and interactive media.* Retrieved from http://www.apa.org/about/policy/inter active-media.pdf

Anderson, C. A., & Bushman, B. J. (2001). Effects of violent video games on aggressive behavior, aggressive cognition, aggressive affect, physiological arousal, and prosocial behavior: A meta-analytic review of the scientific literature. *Psychological Science, 12*(5), 353–359. doi:10.1111/1467-9280.00366

Anonymous. (2006). The broken window theory. *Police Department Disciplinary Bulletin,* 1–3.

Armstrong, D. (2002). *Pathways into and out of crime: Risk, resilience and diversity.* Sheffield, UK: ESRC Research Priority Network.

Armstrong, D. (2003). *Pathways into and out of crime: Risk, resilience and diversity.* Sheffield, UK: ESRC Research Priority Network.

Armstrong, D. (2004). A risky business? Research, policy, governmentality and youth offending. *Youth Justice, 4*(2), 100–116.

Asch, S. E. (1951). Effects of group pressure on the modification and distortion of judgments. In H. Guetzkow (Ed.), *Groups, leadership and men* (pp. 177–190). Pittsburgh, PA: Carnegie Press.

Atkinson, A., Anderson, A., Hughes, K., Bellis, M. A., Sumnall, H., & Syed, Q. (2009). *Interpersonal violence and illicit drugs.* Liverpool: WHO Collaborating Centre for Violence Prevention. Retrieved from http://www.who.int/violenceprevention/ interpersonal_violence_and_illicit_drug_use.pdf

Aubrey, J. S., Hopper, K. M., & Mbure, W. G. (2011). Check that body! The effects of sexually objectifying music videos on college men's sexual beliefs. *Journal of Broadcasting & Electronic Media, 55*(3), 360–379. doi:10.1080/08838151.2011.597469

Ayar, A. A. (2006). Road rage: Recognizing a psychological disorder. *The Journal of Psychiatry & Law, 34*(2), 123–150. doi:10.1177/009318530603400202

Baglivio, M. T., & Epps, N. (2015). The interrelatedness of adverse childhood experiences among high-risk juvenile offenders. *Youth Violence and Juvenile Justice.* doi:10.1177/1541204014566286

Baker, A. M. (2015). Constructing citizenship at the margins: The case of young graffiti writers in Melbourne. *Journal of Youth Studies, 18*, 997–1014.

Baly, M. W., & Cornell, D. G. (2011). Effects of an educational video on the measurement of bullying by self-report. *Journal of School Violence, 10*(3), 221–238. doi: 10.1080/15388220.2011.578275

Bandura, A. (1973). *Aggression: A social learning analysis.* Englewood Cliffs, NJ: Prentice Hall.

Bandura, A. (1977). *Social learning theory.* Englewood Cliffs, NJ: Prentice Hall.

Bandura, A., Barbaranelli, C., Caprara, G. V., & Pastorelli, C. (1996). Mechanisms of moral disengagement in the exercise of moral agency. *Journal of Personality and Social Psychology, 71*(2), 364–374.

Bannister, J., & Kearns, A. (2013). Overcoming intolerance to young people's conduct: Implications from the unintended consequences of policy in the UK. *Criminology and Criminal Justice, 13*(4), 380–397. doi:10.1177/1748895812458296

Barnes, J. C., & Morris, R. G. (2012). Young mothers, delinquent children: Assessing mediating factors among American youth. *Youth Violence and Juvenile Justice, 10*(2), 172–189. doi:10.1177/1541204011423260

Barry, M. (2013). Rational choice and responsibilisation in youth justice in Scotland: Whose evidence matters in evidence-based policy? *The Howard Journal of Criminal Justice, 52*(4), 347–364. doi:10.1111/hojo.12019

Bartol, C. R., & Bartol, A. M. (2009). *Juvenile delinquency and antisocial behaviour* (3rd ed.). Upper Saddle River, NJ: Pearson Prentice Hall.

Barton, A., & Johns, N. (2013). *The policy making process in the criminal justice system.* Abingdon, Oxon: Routledge.

Bateman, T. (2011). Punishing poverty: The 'scaled approach' and youth justice practice. *The Howard Journal of Criminal Justice, 50*(2), 171–183. doi:10.1111/j.1468-2311.2010.00653.x

Baumrind, D. (1967). Child-care practices anteceding three patterns of preschool behavior. *Genetic Psychology Monographs, 75*, 43–88.

Beaver, K. M. (2011). Environmental moderators of genetic influences on adolescent delinquent involvement and victimization. *Journal of Adolescent Research, 26*(1), 84–114. doi:10.1177/0743558410384736

Beaver, K. M., Boutwell, B. B., Barnes, J. C., & Cooper, J. A. (2009). The biosocial underpinnings to adolescent victimization: Results from a longitudinal sample of twins. *Youth Violence and Juvenile Justice, 7*(3), 223–238. doi:10.1177/1541204009333830

Beck, U. (1992). *Risk society: Toward a new modernity.* London: Sage.

Becker, H. (1963). *Outsiders: Studies in the sociology of deviance.* New York, NY: Free Press.

Berry, V., Little, M., Axford, N., & Cusick, G. R. (2009). An evaluation of youth at risk's coaching for communities programme. *The Howard Journal of Criminal Justice, 48*(1), 60–75. doi:10.1111/j.1468-2311.2008.00540.x

Bessant, J., Hill, R., & Watts, R. (2003). *'Discovering' risk: Social research and policy making*. New York, NY: Peter Lang.

Best, J. (2001). *How claims spread: Cross-national diffusion of social problems*. New York, NY: Aldine de Gruyter.

Blackman, S., & Wilson, A. (2014). Psychotic (e)states: Where anti-social behaviour is merged with recreational drug use to signify the social problem group. In S. Pickard (Ed.), *Anti-social behaviour in Britain: Victorian and contemporary perspectives* (p. 293). Houndmills, Basingstoke: Palgrave Macmillan.

Borum, R. (2014). Psychological vulnerabilities and propensities for involvement in violent extremism. *Behavioral Sciences & the Law, 32*(3), 286–305. doi:10.1002/bsl.2110

Bottrell, D. (2009). Dealing with disadvantage: Resilience and the social capital of young people's networks. *Youth & Society, 40*(4), 476–501.

Bottrell, D., Armstrong, D., & France, A. (2010). Young people's relations to crime: Pathways across ecologies. *Youth Justice, 10*(1), 56–72. doi:10.1177/1473225409356758

Bower-Russa, M. E., Knutson, J. F., & Winebarger, A. (2001). Disciplinary history, adult disciplinary attitudes, and risk for abusive parenting. *Journal of Community Psychology, 29*(3), 219–240.

Brazil, A., Matheson, F. I., Doherty, S., & Forrester, P. (2015). A call for help: Women offenders' reflections on trauma care. *Women & Criminal Justice, 25*(4), 241. doi:10.1080/08974454.2014.909760

Briggs, D. B. (2013). Conceptualising risk and need: The rise of actuarialism and the death of welfare? Practitioner assessment and intervention in the youth offending service. *Youth Justice, 13*(1), 17–30. doi:10.1177/1365480212474732

Bronfenbrenner, U. (1979). *The ecology of human development: Experiments by nature and design*. Cambridge, MA:: Harvard University Press.

Brown, A. P. (2004). Anti-social behaviour, crime control and social control. *The Howard Journal, 43*(2), 203–211.

Brunton-Smith, I. (2011). Untangling the relationship between fear of crime and perceptions of disorder: Evidence from a longitudinal study of young people in England and Wales. *British Journal of Criminology, 51*(6), 885–899. doi:10.1093/bjc/azr064

Burney, E. (2005). *Making people behave: Anti-social behaviour, politics and policy*. Cullompton, Devon: Willan Publishing.

Burton, L. J., Westen, D., & Kowalski, R. (2009). *Psychology: 2nd Australian and New Zealand edition*. Brisbane: John Wiley & Sons.

Cabe Space. (n.d.). *Decent parks? Decent behaviour? The link between the quality of parks and user behaviour*. London, UK: Cabe Space. Retrieved from http://web archive.nationalarchives.gov.uk/20110118095356/http:/www.cabe.org.uk/files/decent-parks-decent-behaviour.pdf

Calley, W. (1972). His own story. In J. Baird (Ed.), *From Nuremberg to My Lai* (p. 213). Lexington, MA: D.C. Heath & Co.

Campbell, S. (2002). *Home office research study 236: A review of anti-social behaviour orders*. London: Home Office Research. Retrieved from http://webarchive.nationalar chives.gov.uk/20110314171826/http://rds.homeoffice.gov.uk/rds/pdfs2/hors236.pdf

Carrington, K., & Pereira, M. (2009). *Offending youth: Sex, crime & justice*. Sydney: Federation Press.

Case, S., & Haines, K. (2014). Children first, offenders second positive promotion: Reframing the prevention debate. *Youth Justice, 15,* 229–239. doi:10.1177/1473225414563154

Caspi, A., & Moffitt, T. (1991). Individual differences are accentuated during periods of social change: The sample case of girls at puberty. *Journal of Personality and Social Psychology, 61,* 157–168.

Centers for Disease Control. (2012). *Sexual violence: Facts at a glance.* Retrieved from http://www.cdc.gov/ViolencePrevention/pdf/SV-DataSheet-a.pdf

Cesaroni, C., Downing, S., & Alvi, S. (2012). Bullying enters the 21st century? Turning a critical eye to cyber-bullying research. *Youth Justice, 12*(3), 199–211. doi:10.1177/1473225412459837

Chesney-Lind, M. (1997). *The female offender: Girls, women and crime.* Thousand Oaks, CA: Sage.

Chesney-Lind, M., & Irwin, K. (2008). *Beyond bad girls: Gender, violence and hype.* New York, NY: Rutledge.

Chichetti, D., Toth, S. L., & Rogosch, F. A. (2000). The development of psychological wellness in maltreated children. In D. Chichetti, J. Rappaport, I. Sandler, & R. Weissberg (Eds.), *The promotion of wellness in children and adolescents* (pp. 395–426). Washington, DC: Child Welfare League of America.

Children's Commissioner. (2015). *State of care 2015: What we learnt from monitoring child, youth and family.* Wellington, New Zealand: Office of the Children's Commissioner. Retrieved from http://www.occ.org.nz/assets/Publications/OCC-State-of-Care-2015.pdf

Cohen, S. (1973). *Folk devils and moral panics.* St Albans: Paladin.

Cole, T. B. (2006). Rape at US colleges often fueled by alcohol. *JAMA, 296*(5), 504–505. doi:10.1001/jama.296.5.504

Coleman, J., & Hagell, A. (2007). *Adolescence, risk and resilience: Against the odds.* Chichester, UK: Wiley.

Connell, N. M., Schell-Busey, N. M., Pearce, A. N., & Negro, P. (2014). Badgrlz? Exploring sex differences in cyberbullying behaviors. *Youth Violence and Juvenile Justice, 12*(3), 209–228. doi:10.1177/1541204013503889

Cook, E. C., Pflieger, J. C., Connell, A. M., & Connell, C. M. (2015). Do specific transitional patterns of antisocial behavior during adolescence increase risk for problems in young adulthood? *Journal of Abnormal Child Psychology, 43*(1), 95–106. doi:10.1007/s10802-014-9880-y

Coppock, V., & McGovern, M. (2014). 'Dangerous minds'? Deconstructing counter-terrorism discourse, radicalisation and the 'psychological vulnerability' of Muslim children and young people in Britain. *Children & Society, 28*(3), 242–256. doi:10.1111/chso.12060

Cornford, A. (2012). Criminalising anti-social behaviour. *Criminal Law and Philosophy, 6*(1), 1–19. doi:10.1007/s11572-011-9134-9

Corr, M.-L. (2014). Young people's offending careers and criminal justice contact: A case for social justice. *Youth Justice, 14*(3), 255–268. doi:10.1177/1473225414549695

Cottrell-Boyce, J. (2013). Ending gang and youth violence: A critique. *Youth Justice, 13*(3), 193–206. doi:10.1177/1473225413505382

Cox, A. (2012). New visions of social control? Young people's perceptions of community penalties. *Journal of Youth Studies, 16*(1), 135–150. doi:10.1080/136762 61.2012.697136

Coy, M. (2009). Milkshakes, lady lumps and growing up to want boobies: How the sexualisation of popular culture limits girls' horizons. *Child Abuse Review, 18*(6), 372–383. doi:10.1002/car.1094

Coy, M., & Hovarth, M. A. H. (2011). Lads' mags, young men's attitudes towards women and acceptance of myths about sexual aggression. *Feminism & Psychology, 21*(1), 144–150.

Crawford, A. (2009). Governing through anti-social behaviour: Regulatory challenges to criminal justice. *British Journal of Criminology, 49*(6), 810–831. doi:10.1093/bjc/azp041

Curtis, C. (2006). Sexual abuse and subsequent suicidal behaviour: Exacerbating factors and implications for recovery. *Journal of Child Sexual Abuse, 15*(1), 3–26.

Daw, J. (2001). Road rage, air rage and now 'desk rage': Work stress is leading more people to engage in counterproductive workplace behaviors. *Monitor on Psychology, 32*(7).

DeLisi, M., Vaughn, M. G., Gentile, D. A., Anderson, C. A., & Shook, J. J. (2013). Violent video games, delinquency, and youth violence: New evidence. *Youth Violence and Juvenile Justice, 11*(2), 132–142. doi:10.1177/1541204012460874

Department of Reproductive Health and Research of the World Health Organization, London School of Hygiene and Tropical Medicine, & Council, S. A. M. R. (2013). *Global and regional estimates of violence against women: prevalence and health effects of intimate partner violence and non-partner sexual violence.* Geneva: World Health Organisation.

Deuchar, R. (2010). 'It's just pure harassment … As if it's a crime to walk in the street': Anti-social behaviour, youth justice and citizenship – The reality for young men in the east end of Glasgow. *Youth Justice, 10*(3), 258–274. doi:10.1177/1473225410381686

Donoghue, J. (2008). Antisocial behaviour orders (ASBOs) in Britain: Contextualizing risk and reflexive modernization. *Sociology, 42*(2), 337–355. doi:10.1177/00 38038507087357

Donoghue, J. (2013). Reflections on risk, anti-social behaviour and vulnerable/repeat victims. *British Journal of Criminology, 53*(5), 805–823.

Donzelot, J. (1980). *The policing of families: Welfare versus the state.* London: Hutchinson.

Durkheim, E. (1893 (1984 translation)). *The Division of Labour in Society* (W. D. Halls, Trans.). London, UK: Macmillan.

Durkheim, E. (1951 (original work published 1897)). *Suicide: A study in sociology* (J. A. Spaulding & G. Simpson, Trans.). Glencoe, IL: Free Press.

Eddy, M. J., Reid, J. B., & Curry, V. (2002). The etiology of youth antisocial behavior, delinquency and violence and a public health approach to prevention. In M. R. Shinn, H. M. Walker, & G. Stoner (Eds.), *Interventions for academic and behavior problems* (pp. 27–51). Bethesda, MD: National Association for School Psychologists.

Edmond, T., Auslander, W., Elze, D., & Bowland, S. (2006). Signs of resilience in sexually abused adolescent girls in the foster care system. *Journal of Child Sexual Abuse, 15*(1), 1–28.

Egan, M., Neary, J., Keenan, P. J., & Bond, L. (2012). Perceptions of antisocial behaviour and negative attitudes towards young people: Focus group evidence from adult residents of disadvantaged urban neighbourhoods (Glasgow, UK). *Journal of Youth Studies, 16*(5), 612–627. doi:10.1080/13676261.2012.733809

Englander, E. (2007). *Understanding violence* (3rd ed.). Mahwah, NJ: Lawrence Erlbaum Associates.

Farrington, D. P. (1995). The development of offending and antisocial behaviour from childhood: Key findings from the Cambridge Study, in delinquent development. *Journal of Child Psychology and Psychiatry, 36*, 929–964.

Farrington, D. P. (2015). Prospective longitudinal research on the development of offending. *Australian & New Zealand Journal of Criminology, 48*(3), 314–335. doi:10.1177/0004865815590461

Farruggia, S., Bullen, P., Dunphy, A., Solomon, F., & Collins, E. (2010). *The effectiveness of youth mentoring programmes in New Zealand.* Wellington, New Zealand: Ministry of Youth Development.

Fazel, S., & Danesh, J. (2002). Serious mental disorder in 23 000 prisoners: A systematic review of 62 surveys. *The Lancet, 359*, 545–550.

Fazel, S., Singh, J. P., Doll, H., & Grann, M. (2012). *Use of risk assessment instruments to predict violence and antisocial behaviour in 73 samples involving 24 827 people: systematic review and meta-analysis, BMJ, 345*, e4692–e4692. doi:10.1136/bmj.e4692

Feddes, A. R., Mann, L., & Doosje, B. (2015). Increasing self-esteem and empathy to prevent violent radicalization: a longitudinal quantitative evaluation of a resilience training focused on adolescents with a dual identity. *Journal of Applied Social Psychology, 45*(7), 400–411. doi:10.1111/jasp.12307

Fergusson, D., & Boden, J. (2011). Alcohol use in adolescence. In *Improving the transition: Reducing social and psychological morbidity during adolescence* (pp. 235–256). Auckland, New Zealand: Office of the Prime Minister's Science Advisory Committee.

Fergusson, D. M., Lynskey, M. T., & Horwood, L. J. (1996). Childhood sexual abuse and psychiatric disorders in young adulthood: Part I: The prevalence of sexual abuse and the factors associated with sexual abuse. *Journal of the American Academy of Child and Adolescent Psychiatry, 34*(10), 1355–1364.

Festinger, L., Pepitone, A., & Newcomb, T. (1952). Some consequences of deindividuation in a group. *Journal of Abnormal and Social Psychology, 47*, 382–389.

Fierro, I., Morales, C., & Álvarez, F. J. (2011). Alcohol use, illicit drug use, and road rage. *Journal of Studies on Alcohol and Drugs, 72*(2), 185–193. doi:10.15288/jsad.2011.72.185

Fileborn, B. (2013). *Conceptual understandings and prevalence of sexual harassment and street harassment.* Australian Institute of Family Studies. Retrieved from http://www3.aifs.gov.au/acssa/pubs/sheets/rs6/#publication

Fisher, W. A., & Barak, A. (2001). Internet pornography: A social psychological perspective on internet sexuality. *The Journal of Sex Research, 38*(4), 312–323. doi:10.1080/00224490109552102

Fiske, A. P., & Rai, T. S. (2015). *Virtuous violence*. Cambridge, UK: Cambridge University Press.

Flett, R. A., Kazantzis, N., Long, N. R., MacDonald, C., Millar, M., Clark, B., & Petrik, A. P. (2012). The impact of childhood sexual abuse on psychological distress among women in New Zealand. *Journal of Child and Adolescent Psychiatric Nursing, 25*(1), 25–32. doi:10.1111/j.1744-6171.2011.00311.x

Flood, M. (2009). The harms of pornography exposure among children and young people. *Child Abuse Review, 18*(6), 384–400. doi:10.1002/car.1092

Foubert, J. D., Brosi, M. W., & Bannon, R. S. (2011). Pornography viewing among fraternity men: Effects on bystander intervention, rape myth acceptance and behavioral intent to commit sexual assault. *Sexual Addiction & Compulsivity, 18*(4), 212–231. doi:10.1080/10720162.2011.625552

Foucault, M. (1979). *Discipline and punish: The birth of the prison*. New York, NY: Vintage Books.

Gal, T., & Moyal, S. (2011). Juvenile victims in restorative justice: Findings from the reintegrative shaming experiments. *British Journal of Criminology, 51*(6), 1014–1034. doi:10.1093/bjc/azr052

Gan, S. S., Zhong, C., Das, S., Gan, J. S., Willis, S., & Tully, E. (2014). The prevalence of bullying and cyberbullying in high school: A 2011 survey. *International Journal of Adolescent Medicine and Health, 26*(1), 27–31. doi:10.1515/ijamh-2012-0106

Garland, D. (1985). *Punishment and welfare*. Aldershot: Gower.

Garland, D. (2001). *The culture of control: Crime and social order in contemporary society*. Chicago, IL: University of Chicago Press.

Garnefski, N., & Arends, E. (1998). Sexual abuse and adolescent maladjustment: Differences between male and female victims. *Journal of Adolescence, 21*, 99–107.

Garrett, P. M. (2007). Making 'anti-social behaviour': A fragment on the evolution of 'ASBO politics' in Britain. *British Journal of Social Work, 37*(5), 839–856. doi:10.1093/bjsw/bcl033

Gervilla, E., Cajal, B., & Palmer, A. (2011). Quantification of the influence of friends and antisocial behaviour in adolescent consumption of cannabis using the ZINB model and data mining. *Addictive Behaviors, 36*(4), 368–374. doi:10.1016/j.add beh.2010.12.007

Gibbon, S., Duggan, C., Stoffers, J., Huband, N., Völlm, B.A., Ferriter, M., & Lieb, K. (2010). Psychological interventions for antisocial personality disorder. *Cochrane Database of Systematic Reviews*, Issue 6. Art.No.:CD007668.DOI: 10.1002/14651858.CD007668.pub2

Gibbs, S. (2005). Islam and Islamic extremism: An existential analysis. *Journal of Humanistic Psychology, 45*(2), 156–203. doi:10.1177/0022167805274728

Giddens, A. (1999). Risk and responsibility. *Modern Law Review, 62*(1), 1–10.

Giordano, P. C., Seffrin, P. M., Manning, W. D., & Longmore, M. A. (2011). Parenthood and crime: The role of wantedness, relationships with partners, and ses. *Journal of Criminal Justice, 39*(5), 405–416.

Goldman, L., Giles, H., & Hogg, M. A. (2014). Going to extremes: Social identity and communication processes associated with gang membership. *Group Processes & Intergroup Relations, 17*(6), 813–832. doi:10.1177/1368430214524289

Goldson, B. (2011). *Youth in crisis? Gangs, territoriality and violence*. London, UK: Routledge.

Goode, E., & Ben-Yehuda, N. (2009). *Moral panics: The social construction of deviance* (2nd ed.). Chichester, UK: Wiley.

Goodwin, M. H. (2006). *The hidden life of girls: Games of stance, status, and exclusion,* (Blackwell Studies in Discourse and Culture). Oxford: Blackwell Publishing.

Gormally, S. (2015). 'I've been there, done that …': A study of youth gang desistance. *Youth Justice, 15*(2), 148–165. doi:10.1177/1473225414549679

Gottfredson, M. R., & Hirschi, T. (1990). *A general theory of crime.* Stanford, CA: Stanford University Press.

Graham, G. (2010). Responding to youth crime. In David J. Smith (Ed.), *A new response to youth crime* (pp. 104–142). Cullompton, Devon: Willan Publishing.

Greenberg, D. F., & West, V. (2001). State prison populations and their growth, 1971–1991. *Criminology: An Interdisciplinary Journal, 39,* 615–654.

Griffin, C., Szmigin, I., Bengry-Howell, A., Hackley, C., & Mistral, W. (2013). Inhabiting the contradictions: Hypersexual femininity and the culture of intoxication among young women in the UK. *Feminism & Psychology, 23*(2), 184–206. doi:10.1177/0959353512468860

Hagell, A. (2007). Anti-social behaviour. In J. Coleman & A. Hagell (Eds.), *Adolescence, risk and resilience: Against the odds* (pp. 125–142). Chichester, UK: Wiley.

Haines, K., & O'Mahony, D. (2006). Restorative approaches, young people and youth justice. In B. Goldson & J. Muncie (Eds.), *Youth crime and justice* (pp. 110–124). London, UK: Sage.

Hasinoff, A. A. (2012). Sexting as media production: Rethinking social media and sexuality. *New Media & Society, 5*(4), 449–465. doi:10.1177/1461444812459171

Haydon, D. (2014). Early intervention for the prevention of offending in Northern Ireland. *Youth Justice, 14*(3), 226–240. doi:10.1177/1473225414549693

Hayward, R., & Sharp, C. (2005). *Young people, crime and antisocial behaviour: Findings from the 2003 Crime and Justice Survey.* Retrieved from http://webarchive.nationalarchives.gov.uk/20110220105210/rds.homeoffice.gov.uk/rds/pdfs05/r245.pdf

Heinz, A. J., Beck, A., Meyer-Lindenberg, A., Sterzer, P., & Heinz, A. (2011). Cognitive and neurobiological mechanisms of alcohol-related aggression. *Nat Rev Neurosci, 12*(7), 400–413. doi:10.1038/nrn3042

Hemphill, S. A., Heerde, J. A., Herrenkohl, T. I., & Farrington, D. P. (2015). Within-individual versus between-individual predictors of antisocial behaviour: A longitudinal study of young people in Victoria, Australia. *Australian & New Zealand Journal of Criminology, 48*(3), 429–445. doi:10.1177/0004865815589829

Hendrick, H. (2006). Histories of youth crime and justice. In B. Goldson & J. Muncie (Eds.), *Youth crime and justice* (pp. 3–16). London, UK: Sage.

Hennigan, K., & Spanovic, M. (2012). Gang dynamics through the lens of social identity theory. In F.-A. Esbensen & C. L. Maxson (Eds.), *Youth gangs in international perspective* (pp. 127–149). New York, NY: Springer.

Higgins, G. E., Kirchner, E. E., Ricketts, M. L., & Marcum, C. D. (2013). Impulsivity and offending from childhood to young adulthood in the United States: A developmental trajectory analysis. *International Journal of Criminal Justice Sciences, 8*(2), 182.

Hine, J., France, A., Dunkerton, L., Stubbs, K., Armstrong, D., & Economic and Social Research Council Priority Network. (2012). *Project 1: Risk and resilience in children who are offending, excluded from school or have behaviour problems.* Retrieved from http://www.pcrrd.group.shef.ac.uk/projects/project1/index.htm

Hodgetts, D., Drew, N., Sonn, C., Stolte, O., Nikora, L. W., & Curtis, C. (2010). *Social psychology and everyday life*. Houndmills, Basingstoke: Palgrave Macmillan.

Hodgins, S., De Brito, S. A., Chhabra, P., & Côté, G. (2010). Anxiety disorders among offenders with antisocial personality disorders: A distinct subtype? *Canadian Journal of Psychiatry, 55*(12), 784.

Hodgkinson, S., & Tilley, N. (2011). Tackling anti-social behaviour: Lessons from New Labour for the Coalition Government. *Criminology and Criminal Justice, 11*(4), 283–305. doi:10.1177/1748895811414594

Hogg, M. A., Kruglanski, A., & van den Bos, K. (2013). Uncertainty and the roots of extremism. *Journal of Social Issues, 69*(3), 407–418. doi:10.1111/josi.12021

Hoggan, B. L., & Dollard, M. F. (2007). Effort–reward imbalance at work and driving anger in an Australian community sample: Is there a link between work stress and road rage? *Accident Analysis & Prevention, 39*(6), 1286–1295. doi:10.1016/j.aap.2007.03.014

Holguin, G., & Hansen, D. J. (2003). The "sexually abused child": Potential mechanisms of adverse influences of such a label. *Aggression and Violent Behavior, 8*(6), 645–670.

Holman, B., & Zeidenburg, J. (2006). *Dangers of detention: The impact of incarcerating youth in detention and other secure facilities*. Retrieved from https://www.ncjrs.gov/App/Publications/abstract.aspx?ID=269394

Homans, G. (1961). *Social behavior: Its elementary forms*. New York, NY: Harcourt Brace Jovanovich.

Home Affairs. (2005). *Written evidence: 19. Memorandum submitted by NAPO*. Retrieved from http://www.publications.parliament.uk/pa/cm200405/cmselect/cmhaff/80/80we20.htm

Home Office. (2011). *Ending gang and youth violence: A cross-government report including further evidence and good practice case studies*. Violent and Youth Crime Prevention Unit, Home Office.

Home Office Development and Practice Report. (2004). *Defining and measuring anti-social behaviour*. London, UK: Communication Development Unit. Retrieved from https://www.gov.uk/government/uploads/system/uploads/attachment_data/file/116655/dpr26.pdf

Howell, J. C., & Egley, A. (2005). Moving risk factors into developmental theories of gang membership. *Youth Violence and Juvenile Justice, 3*(4), 334–354. doi:10.1177/1541204005278679

Hughes, G., & Follett, M. (2006). Community safety, youth and the 'anti-social'. In B. Goldson & J. Muncie (Eds.), *Youth crime and justice* (pp. 157–171). London, UK: Sage.

Ireland, T. O., & Smith, C. A. (2009). Living in partner-violent families: Developmental links to antisocial behavior and relationship violence. *Journal of Youth and Adolescence, 38*(3), 323–339. doi:10.1007/s10964-008-9347-y

Jaffee, S., Caspi, A., Moffitt, T. E., Belsky, J. A. Y., & Silva, P. (2001). Why are children born to teen mothers at risk for adverse outcomes in young adulthood? Results from a 20-year longitudinal study. *Development and Psychopathology, 13*(2), 377–397. doi:10.1017/S0954579401002103

Johnson, R. D., & Downing, L. L. (1979). Deindividuation and valence of cues: Effects on prosocial and antisocial behavior. *Journal of Personality and Social Psychology, 37*(9), 1532–1538.

Johnson, P. R., & Indvik, J. (2001). Rudeness at work: Impulse over restraint. *Public Personnel Management, 30*(4), 457.

Jolliffe, D., Farrington, D. P., & Howard, P. (2013). How long did it last? A 10-year reconviction follow-up study of high intensity training for young offenders. *Journal of Experimental Criminology, 9*(4), 515–531.

Jones, T. (2010). Public opinion, politics, and the response to youth crime. In David J. Smith (Ed.) *A new response to youth crime* (pp. 341–379). Cullompton, Devon: Willan Publishing.

Keizer, K., Lindenberg, S., & Steg, L. (2008). The spreading of disorder. *Science, 322*(5908), 1681–1685. doi:10.1126/science.1161405

Kemshall, H. (2002). *Risk, social policy and welfare.* Buckingham, UK: Open University Press.

Kemshall, H. (2008). Risks, rights and justice: Understanding and responding to youth risk. *Youth Justice, 8*(1), 21–37. doi:10.1177/1473225407087040

Kistler, M. E., & Lee, M. J. (2009). Does exposure to sexual hip-hop music videos influence the sexual attitudes of college students? *Mass Communication and Society, 13*(1), 67–86. doi:10.1080/15205430902865336

Klettke, B., Hallford, D. J., & Mellor, D. J. (2014). Sexting prevalence and correlates: A systematic literature review. *Clinical Psychology Review, 34*(1), 44–53. doi:10.1016/j.cpr.2013.10.007

Kochanska, G., Barry, R. A., Stellern, S. A., & O'Bleness, J. J. (2009). Early attachment organization moderates the parent: Child mutually coercive pathway to children's antisocial conduct. *Child Development, 80*(4), 1288–1300. doi:10.1111/j.1467-8624.2009.01332.x

Kochanska, G., & Kim, S. (2012). Toward a new understanding of legacy of early attachments for future antisocial trajectories: Evidence from two longitudinal studies. *Development and Psychopathology, 24*(3), 783–806. doi:10.1017/S0954579412000375

Kreager, D. A., Matsueda, R. L., & Erosheva, E. A. (2010). Motherhood and criminal desistance in disadvantaged neighborhoods. *Criminology, 48*(1), 221–258.

Lachman, P., Roman, C. G., & Cahill, M. (2013). Assessing youth motivations for joining a peer group as risk factors for delinquent and gang behavior. *Youth Violence and Juvenile Justice, 11*(3), 212–229. doi:10.1177/1541204012461510

Laster, K., & Erez, E. (2015). Sisters in terrorism? Exploding stereotypes. *Women & Criminal Justice, 25*(1), 83–99. doi:10.1080/08974454.2015.1023884

Laverty, L., Robinson, J., & Holdsworth, C. (2015). Gendered forms of responsibility and control in teenagers' views of alcohol. *Journal of Youth Studies, 1*–15. doi:10.1080/13676261.2014.992325

Layte, R. (2012). The association between income inequality and mental health: Testing status anxiety, social capital, and neo-materialist explanations. *European Sociological Review, 28*(4), 498–511. doi:10.1093/esr/jcr012

Lemert, E. (1951). *Social pathology.* New York, NY: McGraw-Hill.

Lemert, E. (1967). *Human deviance, social problems and social control.* Englewood Cliffs, NJ: Prentice Hall.

Li, Q. (2006). Cyberbullying in schools: A research of gender differences. *School Psychology International, 27*, 157–170. doi:10.1177/0143034306064547

Little, W., & McGivern, R. (2014). *Introduction to sociology: An Open Textbook Adaptation Story.* Victoria: BC Open.

Loi, N. M., Loh, J. M. I., & Hine, D. W. (2015). Don't rock the boat: The moderating role of gender in the relationship between workplace incivility and work withdrawal. *Journal of Management Development, 34*(2), 169–186. doi:10.1108/JMD-12-2012-0152

Lupton, D. (1999). *Risk: New directions and perspectives.* Cambridge, UK: Cambridge University Press.

Maccoby, E. E., & Martin, J. A. (1983). Socialization in the context of the family: Parent-child interaction. In P. H. Mussen (Ed.) & E. M. Hetherington (Vol. Ed.), *Handbook of child psychology: Vol. 4. Socialization, personality, and social development* (4th ed., pp. 1–101). New York, NY: Wiley.

Macleod, J., Oakes, R., Copello, A., Crome, I., Egger, M., Hickman, M., Oppenkowski, T. & Davey Smith, G. (2004). Psychological and social sequelae of cannabis and other illicit drug use by young people: A systematic review of longitudinal, general population studies. *The Lancet, 363,* 1579–1588.

Martinez-Prather, K., & Vandiver, D. M. (2014). Sexting among teenagers in the United States: A retrospective analysis of identifying motivating factors, potential targets, and the role of a capable guardian. *International Journal of Cyber Criminology, 8*(1), 21.

Massey, S., Cameron, A., Ouellettee, S., & Fine, M. (1998). Qualitative approaches to the study of thriving: What can be learned? *Journal of Social Issues, 54*(2), 337–349.

Mayhew, P., & Reilly, J. L. (2009). The New Zealand crime and safety survey. In *Family Violence Statistics Report.* Wellington, New Zealand: Families Commission.

McAllister, I., & Makkai, T. (2003). Antisocial behaviour among young Australians while under the influence of illicit drugs. *Australian & New Zealand Journal of Criminology, 36*(2), 211–222. doi:10.1375/acri.36.2.211

McAra, L., & McVie, S. (2010). Youth crime and justice: Key messages from the Edinburgh Study of Youth Transitions and Crime. *Criminology and Criminal Justice, 10*(2), 179–209. doi:10.1177/1748895809360971

McAtamney, A., & Morgan, A. (2009). *Key issues in antisocial behaviour.* Research in Practice No. 5. Retrieved from http://www.aic.gov.au/media_library/publications/rip/rip05/rip05.pdf

McCreanor, T., Lyons, A., Griffin, C., Goodwin, I., Moewaka Barnes, H., & Hutton, F. (2013). Youth drinking cultures, social networking and alcohol marketing: Implications for public health. *Critical Public Health, 23*(1), 110–120.

McGee, T. R., Hayatbakhsh, M. R., Bor, W., Aird, R. L., Dean, A. J., & Najman, J. M. (2015). The impact of snares on the continuity of adolescent-onset antisocial behaviour: A test of Moffitt's developmental taxonomy. *Australian & New Zealand Journal of Criminology, 48*(3), 345–366. doi:10.1177/0004865815589828

McLaren, K. (2000). *Tough is not enough – Getting smart about youth crime: A review of research on what works to reduce offending by young people.* Wellington, New Zealand: Ministry of Youth Affairs.

McWhirter, J. J., McWhirter, B. T., McWhirter, E. H., & McWhirter, R. J. (2013). *At-risk youth: A comprehensive response for counselors, teachers, psychologists, and human service professionals* (5th ed.). Belmont, CA: Brooks/Cole.

Mendle, J., Turkheimer, E., & Emery, R. E. (2007). Detrimental psychological outcomes associated with early pubertal timing in adolescent girls. *Developmental Review, 27*(2), 151–171.

Merlo, A. V., & Chesney-Lind, M. (2015). Global war on girls? Policing girls' sexuality and criminalizing their victimization. *Women & Criminal Justice, 25*(1), 71–82. doi: 10.1080/08974454.2015.1026776

Merton, R. K. (1938). Social structure and anomie. *American Sociological Review, 3*(5), 672–682. doi:10.2307/2084686

Milgram, S. (1963). Behavioral study of obedience. *Journal of Abnormal and Social Psychology, 67*(4), 371–378. doi:10.1037/h0040525

Miller, D. W. (2001). Poking holes in the theory of 'broken windows'. *The Chronicle of Higher Education, 47*(22), A14–A16.

Millie, A. (2009). *Anti-social behaviour.* Maidenhead, England: McGraw-Hill.

Ministry of Justice. (2014). *Number of ASBOs made and refused 1999–2013.* London, UK: Ministry of Justice.

Ministry of Justice, Home Office, & the Office for National Statistics. (2013). *An overview of sexual offending in England and Wales.* London, UK: Ministry of Justice, Home Office & the Office for National Statistics. Retrieved from https://www.gov.uk/government/uploads/system/uploads/attachment_data/file/214970/sexual-offending-overview-jan-2013.pdf

Mitchell, K. J., Finkelhor, D., Jones, L. M., & Wolak, J. (2012). Prevalence and characteristics of youth sexting: A national study. *Pediatrics, 129*(1), 13–20. doi:10.1542/peds.2011-1730

Modecki, K. L., Minchin, J., Harbaugh, A. G., Guerra, N. G., & Runions, K. C. (2014). Bullying prevalence across contexts: A meta-analysis measuring cyber and traditional bullying. *Journal of Adolescent Health, 55*(5), 602–611. doi:10.1016/j.jadohealth.2014.06.007

Moffitt, T. E. (1993). Adolescence-limited and life-course persistent antisocial behaviour: A developmental taxonomy. *Psychological Review, 100*(4), 674–701.

Moffitt, T. E. (1994). Natural histories of delinquency. In E. G. M. Weinekamp & H. J. Kerner (Eds.), *Cross-national longitudinal research on human development and criminal behavior* (pp. 3–64). Durdrecht, the Netherland: Kluwer Academic.

Moffitt, T. E. (2006). Life-course-persistent versus adolescent-limited antisocial behavior. In D. Cicchetti & D. J. Cohen (Eds.), *Developmental psychopathology* (2nd ed., Vol. 3, pp. 570–598). Hoboken, NJ: Wiley.

Monsbakken, C. W., Lyngstad, T. H., & Skardhamar, T. (2013). Crime and the transition to parenthood: The role of sex and relationship context. *British Journal of Criminology, 53*(1), 129–148. doi:10.1093/bjc/azs052

Moran, K. (2015). Social structure and bonhomie: Emotions in the youth street gang. *British Journal of Criminology, 55*(3), 556–577. doi:10.1093/bjc/azu085

Morash, M. (2006). *Understanding gender, crime and justice.* Thousand Oaks, CA: Sage.

Muncie, J. (2007a). *Youth & crime* (3rd ed.). London, UK: Sage.

Muncie, J. (2007b). Youth justice and the governance of young people: Global international, national, and local contexts. In S. Venkatesh & R. Kassimer (Eds.), *Youth, globalization, and the law* (pp. 17–56). Stanford, CA: Stanford University Press.

Murdoch, S., Vess, J., & Ward, T. (2010). Descriptive model of the offence process of women violent offenders: Distal background variables. *Psychiatry, Psychology and Law, 17*(3), 368–384. doi:10.1080/13218710903421316

Murdoch, S., Vess, J., & Ward, T. (2011). A descriptive model of female violent offenders. *Psychiatry, Psychology and Law, 19*(3), 412–426. doi:10.1080/13218719.2011.589942

Nardi, F. L., Silvia Mendes da, C., Bizarro, L., & Dell'Aglio, D. D. (2012). Drug use and antisocial behavior among adolescents attending public schools in Brazil. *Trends in Psychiatry and Psychotherapy, 34*(2), 80. doi:10.1590/S2237-60892012000200006

National Collaborating Centre for Mental Health (UK). (2010). *Antisocial personality disorder: Treatment, management and prevention. NICE clinical guidelines, No. 77.* Leicester, UK: British Psychological Society.

New Zealand Family Violence Clearinghouse. (2014). *Data summaries 2014: Snapshot.* Retrieved from http://nzfvc.org.nz/sites/nzfvc.org.nz/files/data-summaries-snapshot-2014.pdf

Office for National Statistics. (2013). *Crime Statistics, Short Story on Anti-Social Behaviour, 2011/12.* Retrieved from http://www.ons.gov.uk/ons/rel/crime-stats/crime-statistics/short-story-on-anti-social-behaviour--2011-12/index.html

Office for National Statistics. (2015). *How much do people binge drink in Great Britain?* Retrieved from http://visual.ons.gov.uk/binge-drinking

Office of the Auditor General (OAG). (2008). *Performance audit report: Mental health services for prisoners.* Wellington, New Zealand: OAG.

Olweus, D. (2012). Cyberbullying: An overrated phenomenon? *European Journal of Developmental Psychology, 9*(5), 520–538. doi:10.1080/17405629.2012.682358

O'Mahony, P. (2009). The risk factors prevention paradigm and the causes of youth crime: A deceptively useful analysis? *Youth Justice, 9*(2), 99–114. doi:10.1177/1473225409105490

O'Rourke, L. (2009). What's special about female suicide terrorism? *Security Studies, 18*, 681–718.

Owens, E. W., Behun, R. J., Manning, J. C., & Reid, R. C. (2012). The impact of internet pornography on adolescents: A review of the research. *Sexual Addiction & Compulsivity, 19*(1–2), 99–122. doi:10.1080/10720162.2012.660431

Oxford University Press. (2015). *Oxford English dictionary.* Retrieved from http://www.oxforddictionaries.com/definition/english/antisocial

Parr, S. (2009). Confronting the reality of anti-social behaviour. *Theoretical Criminology, 13*(3), 363–381.

Patterson, G. R., DeBaryshe, B. D., & Ramsey, E. (1989). A developmental perspective on antisocial behavior. *American Psychologist, 44*(2), 329–335.

Payne, A. A., & Hutzell, K. L. (2015). Old wine, new bottle? Comparing interpersonal bullying and cyberbullying. *Victimization Youth & Society* 0044118X15617401, first published on December 1. doi:10.1177/0044118X15617401

Pezzella, F. S., Thornberry, T. P., & Smith, C. A. (2015). Race socialization and parenting styles: Links to delinquency for African American and White adolescents. *Youth Violence and Juvenile Justice.* doi:10.1177/1541204015581390

Polier, G. G., Herpertz-Dahlmann, B., Matthias, K., Konrad, K., & Vloet, T. D. (2010). Associations between trait anxiety and psychopathological characteristics of children at high risk for severe antisocial development. *ADHD Attention Deficit and Hyperactivity Disorders, 2*(4), 185–193. doi:10.1007/s12402-010-0048-5

Polusny, M. A., & Follette, V. M. (1995). Long-term correlates of child sexual abuse: Theory and review of the literature. *Applied and Preventive Psychology, 4*, 143–166.

Popovici, I., French, M. T., Pacula, R. L., Maclean, J. C., & Antonaccio, O. (2014). Cannabis use and antisocial behavior among youth. *Sociological Inquiry, 84*(1), 131–162. doi:10.1111/soin.12027

Postmes, T., & Spears, R. (1998). Deindividuation and antinormative behavior: A meta-analysis. *Psychological Bulletin, 123*(3), 238–259. doi:10.1037/0033-2909.123.3.238

Powell, A., & Henry, N. (2014). Blurred lines? Responding to 'sexting' and gender-based violence among young people. *Children Australia, 39*(02), 119–124. doi:10.1017/cha.2014.9

Prilleltensky, I., Nelson, G., & Peirson, L. (2001). The role of power and control in children's lives: An ecological analysis of pathways towards wellness, resilience and problems. *Journal of Community and Applied Social Psychology, 11*, 143–158.

Puzzanchera, C., & Sickmund, M. (2008). *Juvenile court statistics 2005*. Pittsburgh, PA: National Center for Juvenile Justice.

Pyszczynski, T., Abdollahi, A., Solomon, S., Greenberg, J., Cohen, F., & Weise, D. (2006). Mortality salience, martyrdom, and military might: The great Satan versus the axis of evil. *Personality and Social Psychology Bulletin, 32*(4), 525–537. doi:10.1177/0146167205282157

Rennison, C. M. (2009). A new look at the gender gap in offending. *Women & Criminal Justice, 19*(3), 171–190. doi:10.1080/08974450903001461

Respect Task Force. (2006). *Respect action plan*. London, UK: Respect Task Force. Retrieved from http://webarchive.nationalarchives.gov.uk/20060116185058/http://homeoffice.gov.uk/documents/respect-action-plan?view=Binary

Richards, K. (2014). Blurred lines: Reconsidering the concept of 'diversion' in youth justice systems in Australia. *Youth Justice, 14*(2), 122–139.

Ringrose, J., Harvey, L., Gill, R., & Livingstone, S. (2013). Teen girls, sexual double standards and 'sexting': Gendered value in digital image exchange. *Feminist Theory, 14*(3), 305–323.

Ritakallio, M., Koivisto, A., von der Bahlen, B., Pelkonen, M., Marttunen, M., & Kaltiala-Heino, R. (2008). Continuity, comorbidity and longitudinal associations between depression and antisocial behaviour in middle adolescence: A 2-year prospective follow-up study. *Journal of Adolescence, 31*, 355–370.

Ritchie, J., & Ritchie, J. (1993). *Violence in New Zealand* (2nd ed.). Wellington, New Zealand: Huia.

Roberto, A. J., Eden, J., Savage, M. W., Ramos-Salazar, L., & Deiss, D. M. (2014). Prevalence and predictors of cyberbullying perpetration by high school seniors. *Communication Quarterly, 62*(1), 97–114. doi:10.1080/01463373.2013.860906

Roberts, L. D., & Indermaur, D. (2005). Social issues as media constructions: The case of 'road rage'. *Crime, Media, Culture, 1*(3), 301–321. doi:10.1177/1741659005057643

Robins, L. N. (1978). Sturdy childhood predictors of adult antisocial behaviour: Replications from longitudinal studies. *Psychological Medicine, 8*(4), 611–622.

Rose, N. (1985) *The psychological complex: Psychology, politics and society in England, 1869–1939*. London: Routledge.

Rose, N. (1999). *Governing the soul: The shaping of the private self* (2nd ed.). London, UK: Free Association Books.

Roskos-Ewoldsen, D. R., & Roskos-Ewoldsen, B. (2005). Applying social psychology to the media. In F. W. Schneider, J. A. Gruman, & L. M. Coutts (Eds.), *Applied social psychology: Understanding and addressing social and practical problems* (pp. 151–178). Thousand Oaks, CA: Sage.

Ross, A., Duckworth, K., Smith, D. J., Wyness, G., & Schoon, I. (2010). *Prevention and reduction: A review of strategies for intervening early to prevent or reduce youth crime and anti-social behaviour.* London, UK: Centre for Analysis of Youth Transitions.

Rutter, M. (2010). Causes of offending and antisocial behaviour. In David J. Smith (Ed.) *A new response to youth crime.* (pp. 180–208). Cullompton, Devon: Willan Publishing.

Sadler, J. (2008). Implementing the youth 'anti-social behaviour' agenda: Policing the Ashton Estate. *Youth Justice, 8*(1), 57–73. doi:10.1177/1473225407087042

Sanders, J., & Munford, P. R. (2007). Speaking from the margins: Implications for education and practice of young women's experiences of marginalisation. *Social Work Education, 26*(2), 185–199.

Sansone, R. A., Lam, C., & Wiederman, M. W. (2010). Road rage: Relationships with borderline personality and driving citations. *The International Journal of Psychiatry in Medicine, 40*(1), 21–29. doi:10.2190/PM.40.1.b

Sansone, R. A., & Sansone, L. A. (2010). Road rage: What's driving it? *Psychiatry (Edgmont), 7*(7), 14–18.

Saucier, G., Akers, L. G., Shen-Miller, S., Kneževié, G., & Stankov, L. (2009). Patterns of thinking in militant extremism. *Perspectives on Psychological Science, 4*(3), 256–271. doi:10.1111/j.1745-6924.2009.01123.x

Scott, S. (2008). An update on interventions for conduct disorder. *Advances in Psychiatric Treatment, 14*(1), 61–70. doi:10.1192/apt.bp.106.002626

Sherif, M. (1958). Superordinate goals in the reduction of intergroup conflict. *American Journal of Sociology, 63,* 349–356.

Sherif, M., Harvey, O. J., White, B. J., Hood, W. R., & Sherif, C. W. (1961). *Intergroup conflict and cooperation: The Robbers Cave experiment.* Norman, OK: University Book Exchange.

Silke, A. (2008). Holy warriors: Exploring the psychological processes of Jihadi radicalization. *European Journal of Criminology, 5*(1), 99–123. doi:10.1177/14773 70807084226

Simmons, R. (2005). *Odd girl out: The hidden culture of aggression in girls.* London, UK: Harcourt.

Simon, R. J. (1975). *Women and crime.* Lexington, MA: Lexington Books.

Skardhamar, T. (2009). Reconsidering the theory on adolescent-limited and life-course persistent anti-social behaviour. *The British Journal of Criminology, 49*(6), 863–878. doi:10.1093/bjc/azp048

Smart, D., Vassallo, S., Sanson, A., & Dussuyer, I. (2004). *Patterns of antisocial behaviour from early to late adolescence.* Canberra: Australian Government. Retrieved from http://www.aic.gov.au

Smart, R. G., Mann, R. E., Zhao, J., & Stoduto, G. (2005). Is road rage increasing? Results of a repeated survey. *Journal of Safety Research, 36*(2), 195–201. doi:10.1016/j.jsr.2005.03.005

Squires, P. (1990). *Anti-social policy: Welfare, ideology and the disciplinary state.* Hemel Hempstead: Harvester Wheatsheaf.

Squires, P., & Stephens, D. E. (2005). *Rougher justice: Anti-social behaviour and young people.* Cullompton, UK: Willan Publishing.

Squires, P., & Stephen, D. (2010). Pre-crime and precautionary criminalisation: Peter Squires and Dawn Stephen look at antisocial behaviour legislation and its role in precautionary criminalisation. *Criminal Justice Matters, 81*(1), 28–29. doi:10.1080/09627251.2010.505405

Stattin, H., Kerr, M., & Bergman, L. R. (2010). On the utility of Moffitt's typology trajectories in long-term perspective. *European Journal of Criminology, 7*(6), 521–545. doi:10.1177/1477370810376573

Staub, E. (2003). *The psychology of good and evil.* New York, NY: Cambridge University Press.

St Cyr, J. L. (2003). The folk devil reacts: Gangs and moral panic. *Criminal Justice Review, 28*(1), 26–46.

Steffensmeier, D., & Allan, E. (1996). Gender and crime: Toward a gendered theory of female offending. *Annual Review of Sociology, 22*, 459–487.

Stephen, D. E. (2009). Time to stop twisting the knife: a critical commentary on the rights and wrongs of criminal justice responses to problem youth in the UK. *Journal of Social Welfare and Family Law, 31*(2), 193–206. doi:10.1080/09649060903043562

Sticca, F., & Perren, S. (2013). Is cyberbullying worse than traditional bullying? Examining the differential roles of medium, publicity, and anonymity for the perceived severity of bullying. *Journal of Youth and Adolescence, 42*(5), 739–750. doi:10.1007/s10964-012-9867-3

Strassberg, D. S., McKinnon, R. K., Sustaíta, M. A., & Rullo, J. (2013). Sexting by high school students: An exploratory and descriptive study. *Archives of Sexual Behavior, 42*(1), 15–21. doi:10.1007/s10508-012-9969-8

Strohmaier, H., Murphy, M., & DeMatteo, D. (2014). Youth sexting: Prevalence rates, driving motivations, and the deterrent effect of legal consequences. *Sexuality Research and Social Policy, 11*(3), 245–255. doi:10.1007/s13178-014-0162-9

Sutherland, E. H. (1924). *Principles of criminology.* Chicago, IL: J. B. Lippincott.

Taheri, S. A., & Welsh, B. C. (2015). After-school programs for delinquency prevention: A systematic review and meta-analysis. *Youth Violence and Juvenile Justice* doi:10.1177/1541204014567542

Tajfel, H., & Turner, J. C. (1979). An integrative theory of intergroup conflict. In W. G. Austin & S. Worchel (Ed.), *The social psychology of intergroup relations* (pp. 33–47). Monterey, CA: Brooks/Cole.

Tannenbaum, F. (1938). *Crime and the community.* New York, NY: Colombia University Press.

Teplin, L. A., Abram, K. M., McClelland, G. M., Mericle, A. A., Dulcan, M. K., & Washburn, J. J. (2006). *Psychiatric disorders of youth in detention.* Washington, DC: U.S. Department of Justice, Office of Justice Programs, Office of Juvenile Justice and Delinquency Prevention.

The Prince's Trust. (2010). *The cost of exclusion: Counting the cost of youth disadvantage in the UK.* London, UK: The Prince's Trust.

The Stationery Office. (2014). Anti-social Behaviour, Crime and Policing Act 2014 Chapter 12. The National Archives. Retrieved from http://www.legislation.gov.uk/ukpga/2014/12/pdfs/ukpga_20140012_en.pdf

Tillfors, M., El-Khouri, B., Stein, M. B., & Trost, K. (2009). Relationships between social anxiety, depressive symptoms, and antisocial behaviors: Evidence from a prospective study of adolescent boys. *Journal of Anxiety Disorders, 23*(5), 718–724.

Ungar, M. (2004). A constructionist discourse on resilience: Multiple contexts, multiple realities among at-risk children and youth. *Youth & Society, 35*(3), 341–365.

Ungar, M. (2012). Introduction to the volume. In M. Ungar (Ed.), *The social ecology of resilience: A handbook of theory and practice* (pp. 1–9). New York, NY: Springer.

US Legal. (2001–2015). *Anti-social behavior law & legal definition.* Retrieved from http://definitions.uslegal.com/a/anti-social-behavior

van der Leun, J., & Koemans, M. (2013). Down these mean streets: An analysis of the local public discourse on antisocial behaviour in disadvantaged urban neighbourhoods in the Netherlands. *Urban Studies, 50*(16), 3342–3359. doi:10.1177/0042098013484180

Van Ouytsel, J., Walrave, M., Ponnet, K., & Heirman, W. (2015). The association between adolescent sexting, psychosocial difficulties, and risk behavior: Integrative review. *The Journal of School Nursing, 31*(1), 54–69. doi:10.1177/1059840514541964

Vermeiren, R., Deboutte, D., Ruchkin, V., & Schwab-Stone, M. (2002). Antisocial behaviour and mental health: Findings from three communities. *European Child & Adolescent Psychiatry, 11*(4), 168–175. doi:10.1007/s00787-002-0275-1

Victoroff, J. (2005). The mind of the terrorist: A review and critique of psychological approaches. *Journal of Conflict Resolution, 49*(1), 3–42. doi:10.1177/0022002704272040

Vivolo-Kantor, A. M., Martell, B. N., Holland, K. M., & Westby, R. (2014). Systematic Review and Content Analysis of Bullying and Cyber-Bullying Measurement Strategies. *Aggression and Violent Behavior, 19*(4), 423–434.

Walgrave, L. (1995). Restorative justice for juveniles: Just a technique or a fully fledged alternative? *The Howard Journal, 34*, 228–249.

Walsh, C. (2011). Youth justice and neuroscience: A dual-use dilemma. *British Journal of Criminology, 51*(1), 21–39. doi:10.1093/bjc/azq061

Wang, J., Nansel, T. R., & Iannotti, R. J. (2011). Cyber and traditional bullying: Differential association with depression. *Journal of Adolescent Health, 48*(4), 415–417. doi:10.1016/j.jadohealth.2010.07.012

Watts, J., Kumar, R., Nicholson, K., Kumar, J., & Youth Council Care to Independence Programme. (2006). Stigma, rights, resilience and stability. *Social Policy Journal of New Zealand*, (27), 12–19.

Weaver, A. J., Zelenkauskaite, A., & Samson, L. (2012). The (non)violent world of YouTube: Content trends in web video. *Journal of Communication, 62*(6), 1065–1083. doi:10.1111/j.1460-2466.2012.01675.x

West, D. J. (1982). *Delinquency: Its roots, careers and prospects.* Aldershot, UK: Gower.

West, D. (2015). An investigation into the prevalence of cyberbullying among students aged 16–19 in post-compulsory education. *Research in Post-Compulsory Education, 20*(1), 96–112. doi:10.1080/13596748.2015.993879

White, R. (2009). Indigenous youth and gangs as family. *Youth Studies Australia, 28*(3), 47–56.

White, R., & Cunneen, C. (2006). Social class, youth crime and justice. In B. Goldson & J. Muncie (Eds.), *Youth crime and justice* (pp. 17–29). London, UK: Sage.

Whitley, B. E., & Kite, M. E. (2006). *The psychology of prejudice and discrimination.* Belmont, CA: Thomson Wadsworth.

Wicherts, J. M., & Bakker, M. (2014). Broken windows, mediocre methods, and substandard statistics. *Group Processes & Intergroup Relations, 17*(3), 388–403. doi:10.1177/1368430213502557

Wilkinson, R., & Pickett, K. (2010). *The spirit level: Why equality is better for everyone.* London, UK: Penguin.

Willott, S., & Lyons, A. C. (2012). Consuming male identities: Masculinities, gender relations and alcohol consumption in Aotearoa New Zealand. *Journal of Community & Applied Social Psychology, 22*(4), 330–345. doi:10.1002/casp.1115

Wilson, H. A., & Hoge, R. D. (2013). Diverting our attention to what works: Evaluating the effectiveness of a youth diversion program. *Youth Violence and Juvenile Justice, 11*(4), 313–331. doi:10.1177/1541204012473132

Wilson, J. Q., & Kelling, G. L. (1982, March). Broken windows: The police and neighborhood safety. *Atlantic Monthly, 249*(3), 29–38.

Wood, W. R. (2015). Why restorative justice will not reduce incarceration. *British Journal of Criminology, 55*(5), 883–900. doi:10.1093/bjc/azu108

World Health Organisation (WHO). (2015). *International statistical classification of diseases and related health problems 10th revision (ICD-10)-2015-WHO version.* Retrieved from http://apps.who.int/classifications/icd10/browse/2015/en#/ F60.2,http://www.who.int/classifications/icd/en

Wyman, P. A., Sandler, I., Wolchik, S., & Nelson, K. (2000). Resilience as cumulative competence promotion and stress protection: Theory and intervention. In D. Chichetti, J. Rappaport, I. Sandler, & R. P. Weissberg (Eds.), *The promotion of wellness in children and adolescents.* Washington, DC: Child Welfare League of America.

Young, T. (2009). Girls and gangs: 'Shemale' gangsters in the UK? *Youth Justice, 9*(3), 224–238. doi:10.1177/1473225409345101

Young, T., Fitzgibbon, W., & Silverstone, D. (2014). A question of family? Youth and gangs. *Youth Justice, 14*(2), 171–185. doi:10.1177/1473225414537569

Youth Justice Board, & Home Office. (2003). *A guide to anti-social behaviour orders and acceptable behaviour contracts.* London, UK: Home Office Communication Directorate.

Zimbardo, P. G. (1969). The human choice: Individuation, reason, and order versus deindividuation, impulse, and chaos. In W. J. Arnold & D. Levine (Eds.), *Nebraska Symposium on Motivation* (Vol. 17, pp. 237–307). Lincoln, NE: University of Nebraska Press.

INDEX